The Symphony Cookbook

The Symphony Cookbook:

America's Heritage in Cookery

Karen Jensen Gibson

Sponsored by the Women's Council, American Symphony Orchestra League

Publisher's Inc.
Del Mar, CA.

Lee Massey, Editor

Frank Arundel, Designer

Library of Congress Catalog Card Number: 76-9249
International Standard Book Number: 0-89163-020-1

Printed in the United States of America
9 8 7 6 5 4 3 2 1

Publisher's Inc.
Del Mar, California 92014

THE WHITE HOUSE

WASHINGTON

    From a look at these delicious recipes, I'm sure many Americans will enjoy the results of "The Symphony Cookbook: America's Heritage in Cookery." I'm so pleased the proceeds will provide money for our American symphony orchestras and for the American Symphony Orchestra League. The joy of music enriches our lives, and private support for our symphonies is crucial.

    What a happy way to support one of the arts.

Best wishes,

Betty Ford

Acknowledgements

My sincere thanks and appreciation to the following people, without whose help this book could not have been written: Mrs. Jay Allen, Mr. Robert C. Bowden, Dr. and Mrs. Paul Palmer (of the Snow Goose Shoppe, La Jolla, California), Mrs. David Girton Fleet, Mr. and Mrs. William C. Karp, Mrs. Samuel Carpenter, Mrs. Colin W. Wied, Dr. and Mrs. Thomas Whitelock III, Mr. and Mrs. Robert Abercrombie Padgett, my Congressman, Bob Wilson, and his Field Representative, Mrs. Marge O'Donnell, Mr. and Mrs. Ralph Pesqueira, Jr., and my editor, Lee Massey.

I am additionally appreciative of the sponsorship of the Women's Council of the American Symphony Orchestra League, its president, Mrs. Robert Hardy Barnes, her board members, and the Symphony women of the United States.

My personal thanks are extended to our First Lady, Mrs. Gerald R. Ford, for her gracious contribution to this book.

Contents

Introduction

If you like to invite friends to dinner parties—and to enjoy these parties yourself—then this book was written especially for you.

My basic recipe for enjoying my own parties can be put into two short words: Plan Ahead. Unless a hostess has made adequate preparations far in advance of the arrival of guests, it is simply not possible to be relaxed and at ease. All of the menus in this book have been designed so that most of the food can be prepared well ahead, leaving the hostess free to share the company of her guests instead of being relegated to the kitchen.

The theme of the book—America's food heritage—reflects my interest in the colonial period. Menus are made up of foods we commonly eat today. Some of the recipes are based on those used in the 1700s, but they have been adapted to today's ingredients and today's methods.

In my own cooking, I prepare Hollandaise sauce and puff paste "from scratch," and use fresh vegetables in preference to those that have been frozen. But many women lack the time for this amount of food preparation. Therefore, many of the recipes included here have been streamlined—but this does not mean that flavor suffers. The recipe for Boeuf Wellington, for example, uses frozen patty shells—yet the result is a gourmet dish that is far more satisfactory than if the cook made the more usual adjustment of substituting plain pie dough for the traditional crust.

As you explore each chapter, you will find that one of the most exciting aspects of our American heritage is not where our individual familial ancestors came from, but rather that our country began with the determined efforts of brave and dedicated patriots, who were united by a common cause—the quest for independence.

I've enjoyed getting together with friends in celebration of some of the important, but not always well-known, events in the history of our country. I hope you'll use this book to do the same!

Karen Jensen Gibson

San Diego, California
June, 1976

To Dean, with my love.

Karen

The adventuresome European explorers who came to North America in the 1600s were seeking gold and riches. What they found along the Eastern Seaboard, instead, was country that showed promise of becoming a land of milk and honey. They stayed to found colonies—the British, Dutch and Swedish in New England, the French along the St. Lawrence River. Distinctly different traditions and lifestyles prevailed, in the thirteen colonies that had been founded by the mid-1700s.

Imagine yourself in the South during this period. In a horse-drawn buggy, you ride along a rutted lane shaded by billowing magnolias with magnificent white blossoms. Along the road are cherry orchards, resplendent with puffed pink blooms, and carefully trimmed gardens with colorful flowers. The green arches of young corn wave in the wind. Huge red-brick plantation homes overlook plots of vegetables—collards, mustard greens, young bean plants, herbs.

In contrast, New England homes of the 1700s are small. Here you travel through rolling countryside where farms and fragrant apple orchards are surrounded by maple woodlands. In each township, neat little white clapboard houses are clustered around a tall-spired but modestly sized church, with the village tavern inn and small shops of craftsmen nearby. Again, food crops form green patterns near the houses.

What would it have been like, to invite to your home the determined patriots who were then setting the stage for the foundation of our country? What foods would the wives of George Washington, Paul Revere, Benjamin Franklin and John Hancock have brought to a potluck dinner party?

Fortunately, I am not today faced with such an illustrious guest list! Instead, I invite twelve couples who are close friends to share potluck fare with us. It's a good way to spread around the labor (and expense) involved in entertaining a crowd. I avoid duplication by enclosing a recipe with the party invitations, asking that each couple provide a specific dish (to be brought either heated or chilled, which simplifies serving problems). The menu is simple. But be sure the friends you select to bring breads have adequate free time to prepare them. (Previous experience with bread-making is not a prerequisite, though— the challenge of a new experience seems to appeal even to those who have never worked with yeast before.) As hostess, I provide the entree—Virginia "Smithfield" Baked Ham. (The genuine Smithfield is available occasionally in stores, or may be ordered specially.)

Overleaf. *Residential street, Williamsburg, Virginia. First settled in 1633, Williamsburg served as capitol of the Colony of Virginia from 1699 to 1780. Reconstruction and preservation of eighteenth-century buildings was begun some half-century ago, through the combined efforts of the Reverend W.A.R. Goodwin, rector of Williamburg's Bruton Parish Church, and John D. Rockefeller, Jr. More than a hundred buildings and homes have been restored, and many are open to the public. Traditional Virginia-style meals are served at the town's three colonial taverns.*

CHAPTER 1

The Thirteen Original Colonies

A Potluck Dinner for Twenty-Four

For this party, I make a big thing of the menu. In advance, I write the name of each dish on a card; these are placed by the appropriate serving dishes as guests arrive with them. Sometimes I also print the menu on a large placard and place it on an easel in the living room—curiosity about the various dishes then builds during the cocktail hour. In the dining room, a bright blue tablecloth and red and white napkins provide a festive touch for my Thirteen Original Colony Potluck dinner. The candlelit buffet table is centered with a plant-filled terrarium, an indoor fern or freshly cut flowers from the garden. To one side are the dinner plates, silver, water glasses and coffee cups. And I always have plenty of coffee for guests to enjoy while the dessert is being served.

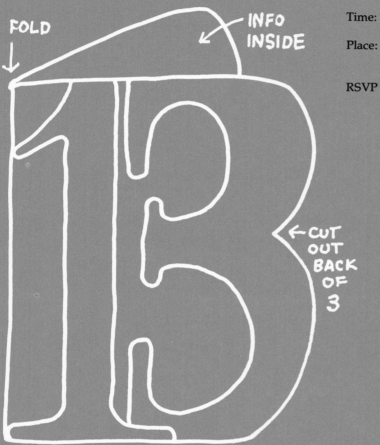

FOLD

INFO INSIDE

← CUT OUT BACK OF 3

Thirteen Colony Potluck Dinner

Foods and customs of the thirteen colonies differed in many ways. You are one of 11 other couples invited to bring specific dishes to our potluck dinner and you might also want to read up on your colony, so you can tell the rest of us about it.

Please bring this dish:

Date:

Time:

Place:

RSVP

MENU

Suggested Wines:

New York Cheddar Crispies
Chablis First Cru 1973
North Carolina Oysters on the Half Shell
Rhode Island Clam Dip with English Biscuits

New Jersey Relish Tray

A Connecticut Tossed Salad with Jamestown Dressing
New Hampshire Cranberry Mold

Virginia Baked "Smithfield" Ham
Chateau Pontet Canet
or
German Lichtenthaler

Boston Baked Beans
Pennsylvania Potatoes
Maryland Green Beans

Delaware Penny Rolls
Massachusetts Brown Bread

Georgia Pecan Pie
Beaulieu Vineyards
Haute Sauterne

South Carolina Coffee

7

Clockwise from Virginia Baked "Smithfield" Ham: Georgia Pecan Pie, New Hampshire Cranberry Mold, Massachusetts Brown Bread, Boston Baked Beans. (Antiques from the private collection of Dr. and Mrs. Paul Palmer.)

Menu

The Cocktail Hour
New York Cheddar Crispies
North Carolina Oysters on the Half Shell
Rhode Island Clam Dip served with English Biscuits

Salads
New Jersey Relish Tray
A Connecticut Tossed Salad with Jamestown Dressing
New Hampshire Cranberry Mold

Entree
Virginia Baked Smithfield Ham

Vegetables
Boston Baked Beans
Pennsylvania Potatoes
Maryland Green Beans

Breads
Delaware Penny Rolls
Massachusetts Brown Bread

Desserts
Georgia Pecan Pie

South Carolina Coffee

New York Cheddar Crispies

2 cups grated sharp Cheddar cheese
½ cup (1 stick) soft butter
1 cup less 2 T. flour
½ tsp. salt
½ tsp. Worcestershire sauce

Combine ingredients with a fork. Form into balls the size of a marble, and place one inch apart on a cookie sheet. Bake 12 to 15 minutes in a preheated 425° oven. Can be frozen and reheated. Makes 5 dozen.

North Carolina Oysters

1 package (3 oz.) whipped cream cheese
   with chives
1 jar (4 oz.) smoked oysters, chopped
1 T. mayonnaise
1 T. dry sherry
½ tsp. onion powder
½ tsp. paprika
Oyster shells

Mix ingredients. Mound the spread on the half shells of large oysters (use on each one an amount about equal to that you would use on four crackers). Garnish with finely chopped chives and serve with your favorite crackers. Makes 1 cup.

Rhode Island Clam Dip

4 slices bacon
1 clove garlic, minced
1 can (7 oz.) minced fancy clams
2 tsp. flour
½ tsp. basil
¼ cup tomato sauce
¼ tsp. salt
⅛ tsp. white pepper
2 tsp. minced fresh parsley
2 T. grated Parmesan cheese

Fry garlic with bacon until bacon is crisp, set aside. Mix remaining ingredients well; add the garlic and crumbled bacon. Serve hot with chips. Makes 1¼ cups.

New Jersey Relish Tray

Arrange the following attractively on a serving tray of crushed ice: carrot sticks, celery sticks, large pitted ripe olives, pickled cauliflower and marinated artichokes. (There are 26 diners, so be sure to have an ample supply.)

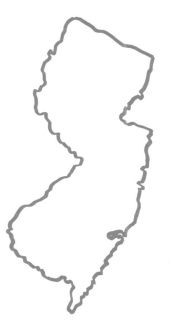

11

A Connecticut Tossed Salad

3 large heads iceberg lettuce, torn in bite-sized pieces
6 green onions, sliced about ¼ inch long (tops and bottoms)
2 bunches red radishes, sliced
½ lb. fresh mushrooms, sliced
4 medium-sized zucchini, sliced about ⅛-inch thick
1 cucumber, sliced
1 green pepper, diced
2 jars (4 oz. each) marinated artichoke hearts, undrained

Combine above ingredients in a very large bowl. Add Jamestown dressing and toss lightly, being careful not to bruise the lettuce.

Jamestown Dressing

1 cup red wine vinegar
1 cup olive oil
¼ cup sesame seed oil
2 large cloves garlic, crushed
1 T. chopped parsley
Pinch each tarragon, basil, rosemary
½ tsp. dry mustard
¼ tsp. onion powder
1 tsp. salt
¼ tsp. black pepper

Combine ingredients in a large glass jar and shake well. Chill before serving.

New Hampshire Cranberry Mold

1 can (13 oz.) crushed pineapple
1 package (6 oz.) lemon Jello
1 cup 7-Up lemon-lime carbonated beverage
½ cup chopped pecans
1 can (1 lb.) whole cranberry sauce

Drain pineapple, reserving liquid. Add enough water to pineapple juice to make 1 cup, heat until boiling. Remove from heat and add Jello, stirring until dissolved; allow to cool. Carefully stir in carbonated beverage; chill until partially set. Add whole cranberry sauce, pineapple and pecans. Pour into bell-shaped pans. When firm, unmold on a lettuce-lined platter. Serves 6.

Virginia Baked "Smithfield" Ham

This recipe calls for the genuine "Smithfield" ham, from razorback hogs. (Although this ham has a distinctive flavor, other varieties of uncooked ham may be substituted.) Scrub ham in hot water, removing the mold and salt. Cover with boiling water and soak 12 hours or overnight. Change the water and simmer over low heat 4 to 5 hours until tender, or until the bone protrudes at least one inch. Let ham cool in the liquid. When cold, remove skin. Put ham in a roasting pan and make criss-cross cuts in the fat on top and sides. Stud with whole cloves and sprinkle with sherry, 2 T. brown sugar, 2 T. cracker meal and pepper. Bake at 425° for 25 minutes, until lightly browned and heated through. Slice paper thin, and serve garnished with crabapples.

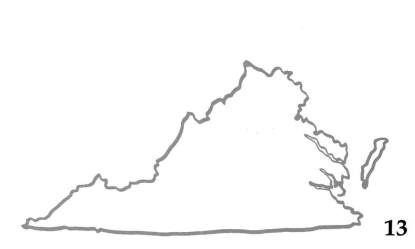

Boston Baked Beans

(Mrs. Ralston King Ailshire)

2 cups dried navy beans
1½ quarts cold water
1 onion
1 tsp. salt
½ lb. lean salt pork
½ cup light molasses
3 T. light brown sugar
1 tsp. dry mustard
1 T. catsup

Cover cleaned beans with water. Bring to boil for 2 minutes, cover pan and remove from heat. Let stand 1 hour, then cook until tender. (If water gets too low, add more.) After beans are tender, drain (reserving liquid). Place in a bean pot. Cut the salt pork in half, then make 1-inch-deep cuts across each half. Bury the onion and the salt pork in the beans. Mix 1½ cups bean liquid with the remaining ingredients, and pour this mixture over the beans. Add enough liquid to cover. Place cover on crock and bake in oven at 300° for 8 hours; uncover for the last hour. Serves 8.

Pennsylvania Potatoes

8 large sweet potatoes
1½ cups light brown sugar
½ cup (1 stick) butter
¼ cup pineapple juice

Cook sweet potatoes in boiling salted water until done; peel. Cut in half crosswise, then cut pieces in half again lengthwise. Place in buttered 9x13-inch glass baking dish. Sprinkle evenly with brown sugar, dot with butter and pour pineapple juice over top. Bake in a preheated oven at 400° for at least 30 minutes. Serves 12.

14

Maryland Green Beans

Cook four 10-ounce packages frozen green beans according to directions, and serve with the following sauce:

2 T. butter
2 T. flour
¾ cup buttermilk
2 T. yoghurt
¼ cup sour cream
2 T. water
¼ tsp. salt
½ cup grated Parmesan cheese
½ cup salted roasted peanuts
¼ cup finely sliced green onion tops

Melt butter, stir in flour and cook gently for a few minutes. Gradually blend in the buttermilk, then the yoghurt, sour cream, water, salt and green onion tops. Fold in the grated cheese and heat until cheese is melted. Stir in the peanuts. Pour sauce over the cooked green beans. Serves 8.

Delaware Penny Rolls

(Mildred Ailshire Jensen)

1½ packages active dry yeast
3 T. sugar
1 tsp. salt
4 T. shortening
1 cup skim milk, scalded
3½ cups flour
1 egg, slightly beaten

Dissolve yeast in water and put aside. Place sugar, salt and shortening in a bowl; add scalded milk to melt the shortening, and let cool. Add 1 cup flour, egg and yeast. Mix. Add remaining flour and beat well by hand. Cover and let rise in warm place (out of drafts) until double in bulk. Turn out on a lightly floured board and shape into small balls. Place 3 balls in each well-greased muffin cup. Cover and let rise again until double, then bake in preheated oven at 400° for about 12 minutes. Serve hot with butter balls. Makes 24 rolls.

15

Massachusetts Brown Bread

¼ cup graham flour
1¾ cups coarse wheat flour
1 cup sifted all-purpose flour
1 cup yellow cornmeal
3 T. sugar
1 tsp. salt
1½ tsp. baking powder
¾ tsp. baking soda
¼ cup dark molasses
1 egg
2 cups buttermilk
⅔ cup seedless raisins

Mix together flours, cornmeal, sugar, salt, baking powder and baking soda. Add molasses and remaining ingredients, and mix well. Half fill three greased 1-lb. coffee cans with mixture, or fill a large greased mold two-thirds full. Cover tightly and place on rack in a large pan containing boiling water; cover pan and steam for 3 hours. Uncover molds and place in a 400° oven for 7–10 minutes to dry slightly. Remove bread from molds, slice and serve. Serves 8.

Georgia Pecan Pie

(Rosalee Pesqueira)

3 eggs, slightly beaten
1 cup white sugar
1 cup light corn syrup
2 T. melted butter
1 tsp. vanilla
¼ tsp. salt
1½ cup chopped pecans
Unbaked 9-inch pie shell

Beat eggs slightly in medium-sized bowl. Beat in sugar; blend in corn syrup, butter, vanilla, salt and pecans. Pour into unbaked pie shell. Bake in preheated oven at 400° for 15 minutes; reduce heat to 350° and bake 35–40 minutes, until brown and slightly puffed. Cool before serving. Serves 8.

South Carolina Coffee

Add 1 oz. bourbon whiskey or apricot brandy to your favorite coffee during the perking process. Delicious!

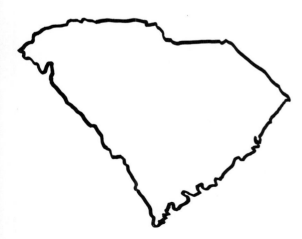

Abigail Adams, the only woman in history to become the wife of a President and the mother of one as well, was very much ahead of her time. She specifically asked her husband to see to it that the Constitution stated that women were to be given the right to vote. "Remember the ladies, John!" she told him. (He did not, and, since the document said nothing on this score, for nearly 140 years women were banned from sharing the voting rights of male citizens.)

John and Abigail Adams, who loved one another dearly, were separated for long periods during the ten years he devoted to serving Congress and to diplomatic missions in Europe. Life in the colonies, at this time, was primarily concerned with survival. Adams visited Paris in 1780 and wrote that there were many things he'd like to investigate, but added, "My duty is to study geography, navigation, commerce and agriculture in order to give my children a right to study philosophy, painting, poetry, music, architecture, sculpture, tapestry and porcelain."

Music, in particular, was in short supply in the colonies. There were not, in this new land, kings and counts such as those who traditionally supported private court orchestras in Europe. And the colonial churches had been founded by people who objected to the ostentatious ceremonies of European religions. Although public concerts were presented in Boston, New York and Charleston as early as the 1730s, not until 1800 was there enough wealth to support regular musical performances in the major cities.

Overleaf. *Interior view, Faneuil Hall, Boston, Massachusetts. This colonial building, erected by merchant Peter Faneuil as a market-place and meeting hall, and presented by him to the city in 1742, is called the "Cradle of Liberty" because of its use as a meeting place by Revolutionary patriots. Today it houses a library and a military museum, as well as an impressive display of Revolutionary paintings. At the hall's street level, goods are still sold from open stalls, much as they were in colonial times.*

CHAPTER 2

Abigail and John Adams

A Pre-Symphony Buffet

Today, almost everyone in the United States lives within range of the sound of a symphony. Orchestras are supported not only in major urban centers but in smaller communities as well, and they are common at colleges and universities.

A pre-symphony buffet is a practical idea, because it is difficult for most of us to fit in dinner before the concert. Presenting an attractive array of food and allowing guests to serve themselves is a gracious way to diminish the time devoted to dining. I keep decorations for my pre-symphony buffets plain and simple. We usually begin at 6 sharp, which allows plenty of time for us to reach the concert hall at 8 or 8:30. This menu is particularly fitting—much of the food is "finger-food," and the dishes are not "heavy."

A Pre-Symphony Buffet

Come to our pre-symphony buffet, which is being dedicated to Abigail and John Adams. Because of their letters, we know much about life in colonial times. We'll toast them, as well as the evening of music that will follow!

Date:

Time:

Place:

RSVP

FOLD

PRINT
INFO
INSIDE

Dear John

CUT
OUT
SHAPE

MENU

Spicey Vegetable Dip
Clam Dip
Teriyaki Steak Appetizer
Chicken Liver Boats
Filled Cornucopias
Skewered Shrimp and Bacon

Beef Salad Abigail

Salmon Loaf
Turkey à la King

Election Cake

Claret Sangaree

Clockwise from upper right: Skewered Shrimp and Bacon, Wheel of Brie Cheese, Crackers, John's Favorite Cake, Turkey à la King, Hot Buttered Noodles.

Spicey Vegetable Dip

½ cup sour cream
½ cup yoghurt
1 package (8 oz.) cream cheese
1 tsp. seasoned salt
1 T. beer
2 T. green onion, chopped
1 tsp. parsley, chopped
3 T. pimento, chopped
1 tsp. paprika
Vegetable sticks

Combine ingredients for dip and blend well. Serve in bowl surrounded by attractively arranged vegetable sticks.

Clam Dip

1 small can chopped clams
4 T. mayonnaise
1 T. lemon juice
⅛ tsp. celery salt
3 drops liquid red-pepper seasoning
2 packages (3 oz. each) cream cheese, at room temperature
1 T. chopped chives
1 T. chopped olives
Unsalted crackers

Drain clams. Mix mayonnaise and lemon juice, season with garlic salt and red-pepper seasoning. Beat cheese until smooth, then mix thoroughly with mayonnaise mixture. Add chives, olives and clams, and beat until well blended. Chill and serve with crackers.

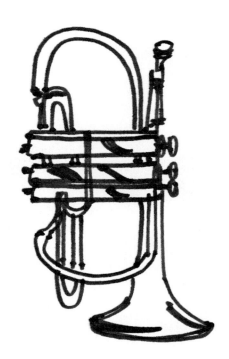

Teriyaki Steak Appetizer

1 lb. filet mignon
1 bottle Kikkoman Teriyaki sauce
Fresh garlic
1 can water chestnuts

Rub filets with garlic. Cut meat into pieces ½ to ¾ inch wide. Put teriyaki sauce in a plastic bag with meat and marinate overnight. Skewer meat on bamboo sticks, top with half a water chestnut and place under broiler until done (about 7 minutes), turning to cook evenly.

Chicken Liver Boats

Coat 8 oz. chicken livers with 2 T. flour. Cook with 2 T. butter, 2 T. chopped onion and ½ tsp. steak sauce for 10 minutes. Add ¼ tsp. salt and dash of pepper; mash livers well. Stir in ¼ cup light cream. Prepare 1 stick pie crust mix, roll out and cut in 2¼-inch rounds. Place 1 tsp. liver mixture on each round, pinching ends to form "boats." Sprinkle with Parmesan cheese. Bake at 425° for 10 minutes. Sprinkle with paprika before serving. Makes 12.

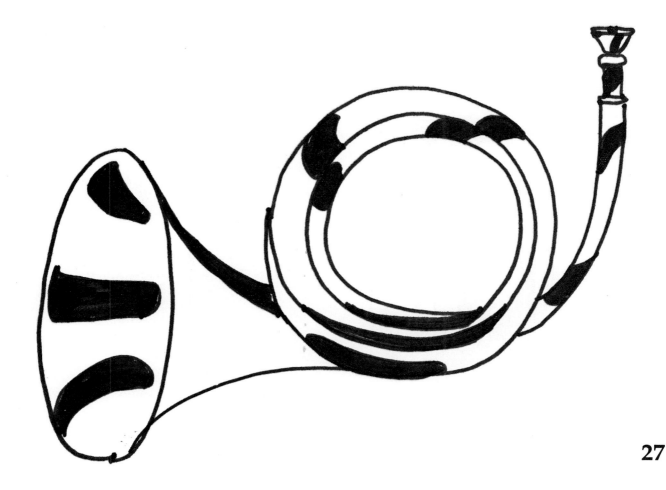

Filled Cornucopias

3 oz. cream cheese with chives
½ cup whipped cottage cheese
2 T. minced parsley
2 T. pimento, chopped
½ tsp. dillweed
½ tsp. seasoned salt
16 slices small salami
Pimento and parsley for garnishing

Blend cream cheese and cottage cheese, add parsley, chopped pimento and seasonings. Roll salami into cornucopias and fasten with toothpicks. Fill each cornucopia with cheese mixture, using a small spoon. Garnish with a dot of pimento and sprig of parsley. Makes 16 slices.

Skewered Shrimp and Bacon

18 shrimp, shelled and deveined
2 T. olive oil
1 T. lemon juice
Salt and pepper to taste
½ tsp. paprika
18 small strips bacon

Marinate shrimp for several hours in oil, lemon juice and seasonings. Drain. Wrap each shrimp in bacon strip, securing with wet toothpick. Broil, turning frequently, until bacon is crisp and shrimp are bright pink. Makes 18.

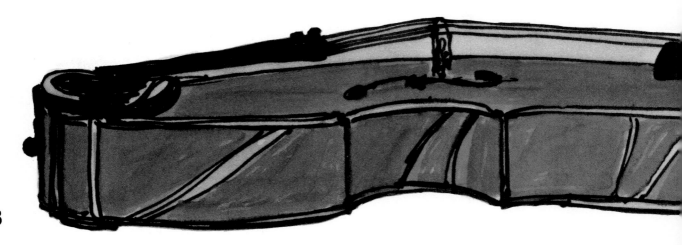

Beef Salad Abigail

5 lbs. beef short ribs
¼ cup chopped carrot
½ cup chopped onion
¼ cup olive oil
¼ cup red-wine vinegar
½ tsp. dry mustard
½ tsp. salt
Dash cayenne
1 medium red onion, sliced in rings and
    separated
½ sweet red pepper, cut in matchsticks
3 medium carrots, in matchsticks
3 stalks celery, in matchsticks
2 T. cut celery leaves

Cover short ribs, carrot and onion with salted water and bring to a boil. Cover and simmer until tender (1½ to 2 hours). Remove meat from liquid, strip from bone and trim off fat. Cut meat in matchsticks (there will be about 3 cups) and chill. Combine olive oil, vinegar, mustard, salt and cayenne in jar and shake well. Chill. Shake again before using. To serve, combine beef, onion, pepper, carrot and celery sticks, and toss with dressing. Sprinkle with cut celery leaves. Serves 6.

Salmon Loaf

1 package lemon gelatin
1 cup boiling water
½ cup cold water
3 T. vinegar
½ cup mayonnaise (or salad dressing)
¼ tsp. salt
2 cups cooked salmon (fresh or canned),
    flaked
½ cup chopped celery
2 T. chopped parsley
¼ cup chopped onion

Dissolve gelatin in boiling water. Add cold water, vinegar, mayonnaise and salt, and beat well. Chill until almost firm, then beat until fluffy. Fold in remaining ingredients and pour into loaf pan (8½x4½x2½ inches). Chill until set. Unmold on crisp greens. Serves 6.

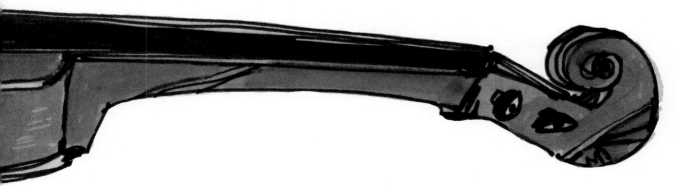

White and Red Bean Salad

1 cup dried white beans, washed and drained
1 cup dried red kidney beans, washed and drained
6 cups water
2 T. olive oil
½ tsp. ground sage
2 garlic cloves
1½ tsp. salt
Dash cayenne
¾ tsp. paprika
¼ cup cider vinegar
1 T. tarragon vinegar
¼ cup minced green pepper
2 T. chopped dill pickle
3 sprigs parsley, chopped
2 T. dried chives
Romaine
2 pimentos cut in strips for garnish

Cover beans with water, bring to boil, boil 2 minutes. Cover pan and let stand 1 hour. Add oil, sage and garlic, and cook until beans are tender (adding more water if necessary). Drain, remove garlic and cool. Add remaining ingredients except romaine and pimento; mix well and chill. Serve in bowl lined with romaine, garnish with pimento. Serves 8.

Turkey à la King

Make a white wine sauce as for Seafood Medley (page 238). To heated sauce add 4 cups cooked turkey (cubed), ½ lb. fresh sautéed mushrooms, 1 package (10 oz.) frozen peas. Heat gently until peas are tender. Serve over buttered noodles or parsleyed rice. Serves 8.

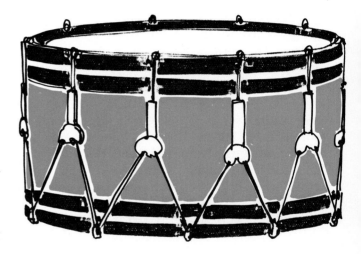

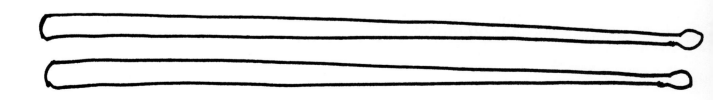

Election Cake

2 packages active dry yeast
¼ cup very warm water
1 tsp. granulated sugar
½ cup boiling water
½ cup dark brown sugar
1¼ cups unsifted all-purpose flour
1 cup granulated sugar
2¾ cups sifted cake flour
1 tsp. salt
1 tsp. nutmeg
½ tsp. mace
3 eggs
¾ cups shortening
½ tsp. grated lemon rind
1 tsp. vanilla extract
½ cup milk
½ cup dried currants
½ cup diced candied pineapple
½ cup diced citron
¼ cup diced candied orange peel

Sprinkle dry yeast into warm water. Let stand for a few minutes, then stir until dissolved. Add sugar and let stand until frothy (5 to 10 minutes). Pour boiling water over brown sugar, then let cool to lukewarm; add yeast and unsifted flour, and beat until smooth. Cover and let rise for 30 minutes. After 20 minutes, sift 1 cup granulated sugar, cake flour, salt and spices into a large bowl. Add remaining ingredients except fruit, and beat for 3 minutes. Add yeast mixture and beat for 1 minute, then add fruit. Let rise in greased 9-inch tube pan until light (about 1 hour). Bake in preheated 350° oven for 50 to 60 minutes. Cool for 20 minutes in pan, then invert on rack. Frost when cool.

Pineapple Frosting

Mix 1 T. pineapple juice, 1 T. light cream, 1 T. butter in a bowl; heat over hot water until melted. Add ¼ tsp. *each* grated orange and lemon rind, and ½ cup sifted confectioner's sugar. Beat until smooth. Add 2 T. minced candied pineapple. Spoon frosting over cake, letting it run down sides.

Claret Sangaree

1 tsp. sugar
1 oz. lemon juice
6 oz. Claret (Cabernet Sauvignon)

Combine ingredients and pour into a glass filled with crushed ice; stir. Garnish with freshly grated nutmeg. Serves 1.

XV VX. PROCLAIM L

LADA. BY ORDER OF

SS AND STOW

PHILADA

MDCCLIII

The year 1752 was a joyous one in Philadelphia. Fifty years earlier, founder William Penn had granted his Quaker colony a democratic constitution, and this anniversary brought with it widespread celebration. A special bell had been ordered from London, at a cost of $300 (a small fortune, in those times). Inscribed on it was a Biblical quotation, "Proclaim Liberty throughout all the land unto all the inhabitants thereof."

But the huge bell, weighing more than a ton, proved to be brittle. While it was being tested, it cracked. The Philadelphians, stubbornly determined to have their symbol of liberty, had it twice recast. It was rung every year on the anniversary of the adoption of the Declaration of Independence. Then, on July 8, 1835, it cracked once more, as it was tolling the death of Chief Justice John Marshall.

The Liberty Bell can still be seen in Philadelphia. It is no longer rung, but has become one of our most significant symbols of liberty and freedom—a reminder of the courage, dedication and sacrifices made by our colonial forebears.

A Liberty Bell brunch is one of my favorite parties. When guests arrive, at 10:30 or 11 in the morning, I'm ready to pour icy champagne over some frosted strawberries. Days ahead, I've prepared an assortment of breakfast pastries. (If you don't enjoy baking, these can be purchased at a bakery—but *do* avoid the tasteless variety sold in packages.)

In my invitations, I ask guests to come "with bells on"—and they certainly do! They arrive wearing Indian bells, bells from "Santa Claus' sleigh"—and one year a gentleman turned up with a large cowbell dangling from his neck.

Overleaf. *Liberty Bell. The famed symbol of the American Revolution is now displayed in a special pavilion at Independence National Historical Park, Philadelphia, Pennsylvania.*

I use my own favorite bells as a centerpiece for the table, and surround them with greenery. The Eggs Benedict are served with all the flair they deserve, accompanied by the traditional broiled tomatoes. Colorful fruits mingle together in the berry bowl, ready to be topped with cool whipped cream. Brioche can be a pain, but the simplified recipe given here is easy.

Eggs Benedict is rather tricky to prepare—should you find the need of a little help in the kitchen, by all means ask a guest to help you. Never allow yourself to be a rushed and nervous hostess!

CHAPTER 3

Liberty Bell Party

A Weekend Brunch

Clockwise from upper right: Hot Brioche, Eggs Benedict with Broiled Tomatoes, Berry Bowl Chantilly, Champagne.

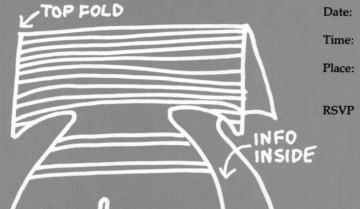

You Are Invited to a Liberty Bell Brunch

"Give me liberty or give me death!"—Patrick Henry

The Liberty Bell, sent to Philadelphia from England in 1752, cracked immediately. Recast, it cracked again in 1825, on being rung for the funeral of Chief Justice John Marshall.

Let the bell resound! Come to brunch—with your bells on!

Date:

Time:

Place:

RSVP

38

MENU

Champagne
Silver Fizz

Berry Bowl Chantilly

Hot Brioche with Sweet Butter
Assorted Pastries

Eggs Benedict

Broiled Tomatoes

Coffee and Tea

Champagne

Before pouring the champagne, prepare a dish of powdered sugar and a bowl of large-stemmed strawberries. Dip the strawberries into the sugar, and then float one berry in each champagne glass.

Silver Fizz

1 oz. lemon juice
2 tsp. sugar
White of 1 egg
2 oz. gin or vodka
4 oz. crushed ice

Blend ingredients in a blender or mixing machine for 30 seconds. Pour into a 10-oz. glass and add soda water to fill. Serves 1.

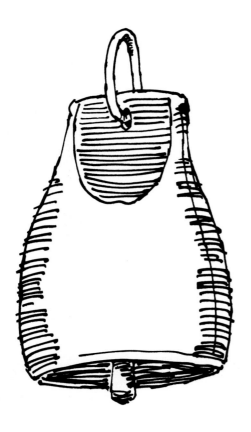

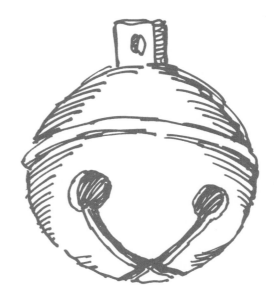

Brioche

1 package (13¾ oz.) hot roll mix
3 egg yolks
2 T. sugar
½ tsp. grated lemon peel
1 egg white, slightly beaten
1 T. sugar

Soften yeast from roll mix in ⅔ cup water. Add 1 cup of the mix, egg yolks, 2 T. sugar and lemon peel. Beat 3 minutes at high speed with electric mixer. With wooden spoon, gradually stir in remaining roll mix, blending well. Place in greased bowl and cover. Refrigerate 2 hours or overnight. Turn out onto lightly floured surface. Divide dough into four equal parts. Form one portion into 9 small balls; divide each of the other three portions into 3 balls. Place 1 large ball in each greased custard cup or individual soufflé dish and make an indentation in the top. Press one of the smaller balls into each indentation. Cover and let rise in warm place until double in bulk (35 to 40 minutes). Combine egg white and 1 T. sugar, and brush tops of rolls with this mixture. Bake in preheated oven at 375° about 15 minutes. Serve warm. Makes 9 rolls.

Berry Bowl Chantilly

In an attractive bowl, combine fresh or frozen whole strawberries, raspberries and blackberries. Sprinkle with sugar and serve with topping, prepared by whipping 1 cup of cream and adding ½ tsp. vanilla and 2 T. sugar.

Assorted Pastries

These may be rolls you make yourself or purchase at your local bakery. Just make sure you provide a varied—and colorful—choice.

Eggs Benedict

6 English muffins, split
1 lb. Canadian bacon
12 eggs
1 can (⅞ oz.) truffles, or black olives thinly sliced
1 pkg. hollandaise sauce mix

Warm the muffins. Fry bacon until browned but not too crisp. Prepare hollandaise sauce. Poach eggs. Place muffins on a serving platter, and top them with bacon. Put an egg atop the bacon on each muffin. Cover with hollandaise and garnish with sliced truffles or olives. Serves 6.

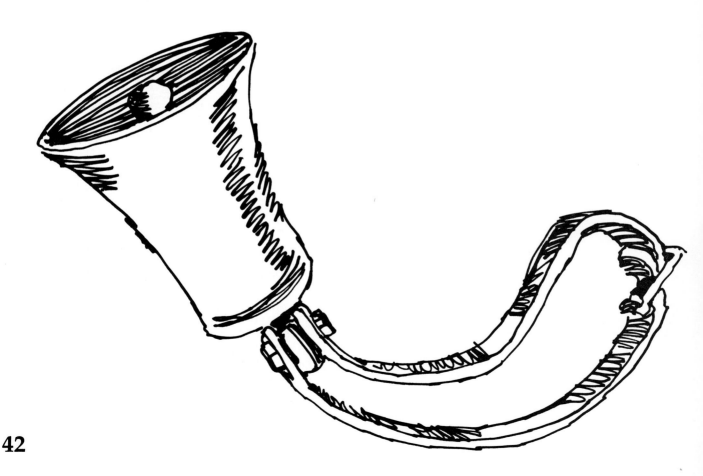

Broiled
Tomatoes

Wash 6 medium-sized tomatoes, neatly slice off stem ends and discard. Dot each tomato with ½ tsp. butter and season with salt and pepper to taste. Sprinkle with chopped parsley. Broil 5 minutes until tops of tomatoes are golden brown.

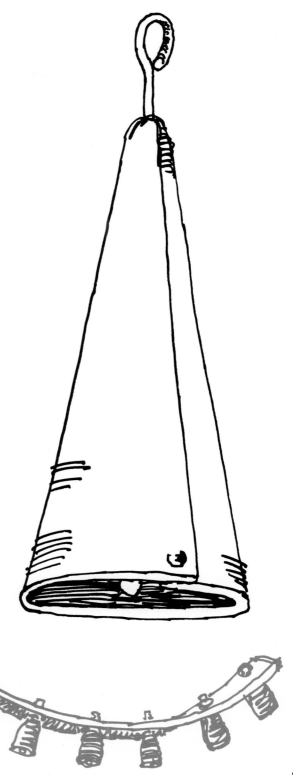

43

Washington's Birthday is one of our country's most venerable holidays—it was celebrated for the first time the first year he was in office. Washington's family was by that time already firmly established in America. John Washington, George's great-grandfather, had been a mate on an English vessel that ran aground in the Potomac in the late 1650s; he fell in love with a Virginia woman, married her, and settled at a place called Ferry Farm (the present site of Mount Vernon). George was born three generations later, in 1732. At the age of 15 he became a surveyor (also the profession of his father).

At 27 Washington married Martha Dandridge Custis, a widow eight years his senior. Social life at Mount Vernon, which had grown to a 40,000-acre plantation, included wild-game hunting, duck shooting, fox hunting and fishing—a gracious life that was unfortunately interrupted by political turmoil. Ben Franklin wrote in 1776, "We must all hang together, or assuredly we shall all hang separately." Washington set out at the head of the Continental Army to do battle with English forces, but not until 1781 did the surrender of British general Cornwallis at Yorktown bring the Revolutionary War to a close.

In 1789, after the new nation's first election, the Washingtons moved to the Presidential House in Philadelphia. Here the first "First Couple" faced the responsibility of entertaining European royalty. Fortunately, they had been entertaining elaborately for years, sometimes with dinners including as many as 32 courses.

Our first President loved fine parties. His accounts show that he sometimes ordered as many as 26 dozen bottles of claret and champagne at one time. At Mount Vernon, dinner was always at 4 o'clock. Guests were entertained lavishly—one gentleman who was invited for dinner liked the accommodations so well that he remained for the rest of his life! Although the Washingtons lived well, most of their funds went toward the upkeep of their plantation, which was the home of numerous relatives as well as some 150 servants.

Overleaf. *Dining room, Mount Vernon, Virginia. At the age of 22, George Washington inherited Mount Vernon plantation from his half-brother Lawrence. The plantation house, then a relatively modest one-and-a-half story structure, had been built in 1743. Prior to marrying Martha Custis, Washington added another story, and in 1787 wings were extended at either end of the mansion. The estate, long neglected, was rescued from oblivion in 1858 by Miss Ann Pamela Cunningham, who founded The Mount Vernon Ladies' Association. This organization restored the Washington plantation and continues to maintain it today.*

CHAPTER 4

George Washington's Birthday

A Plan-Ahead Casserole Party

Whichever date you wish to observe, Washington's Birthday remains a fine reason for celebration. I sometimes send invitations that include one of his favorite sayings: "Gentlemen . . . I have a cook who never asks whether company has come, but whether the hour has come." (He once said it was a rare evening when he and Martha had the privilege of dining alone.)

One year, I presented each male guest with an inexpensive white wig (from a dime store) and each woman with a small fan. For a real gala, you might ask guests to wear Colonial costumes.

As friends arrive, I offer them Swiss Smoky Beef Puffs and a decorative Relish Tree in the living room—just enough to whet their appetites for the Filet of Sole casserole prepared the day before. At this party, I usually serve a non-alcoholic punch.

But let's get on with the party!

Clockwise from top: Stuffed Filet of Sole with Lobster and Wine Sauce, White and Wild Rice Croquettes, French Broccoli Ring, Cherry Parfait with Ladyfingers.

George Washington's Birthday Party

1732-1799
George Washington, born the son of a wealthy landowner/ surveyor in Virginia, took up the same occupation as his father. Later he fought bravely as a soldier in the French and Indian War and the Revolutionary War. Help us celebrate the birthday of our nation's first President!

Date:

Time:

Place:

"Gentlemen . . . I have a cook who never asks whether the company has come, but whether the hour has come."—George Washington

FOLD

PRINT INFO INSIDE

CUT OUT

50

MENU

Suggested Wines:

Swiss Smoky Beef Puffs
Relish Tree with Winter Dip
Individual Steak and Kidney Pies

Beaujolais Villages
Louis Jadot

Fresh Spinach Salad with Green Goddess Dressing

Stuffed Filet of Sole with Lobster and Wine Sauce   1970 Pouilly Fuissé
Louis Jadot

White and Wild Rice Croquettes
French Broccoli Ring
Spiced Pears

Crescent Rolls

Cheese and Fruit Bowl
Cherry Parfait with Ladyfingers

Madeira
Rainwater Wicker 1919

Coffee or Tea

Swiss Smoky Beef Puffs

Puffs:

1 cup boiling water
½ cup butter
½ tsp. salt
¾ cup plus 2 T. flour
4 eggs
½ cup shredded processed Swiss cheese

Combine butter and boiling water in saucepan, cook over low heat until butter melts. Add flour and salt, stir vigorously. Continue to cook, stirring constantly, until mixture forms a smooth ball and leaves the sides of the pan. Remove from heat. Add eggs one at a time, beating vigorously after each; continue beating until smooth. Stir in Swiss cheese. Drop the dough onto a greased baking sheet, using one *level* teaspoon for each puff. (These puffs may seem very small, but they expand in baking and are a perfect size for filling as an appetizer.) Bake in a moderate oven (375°) for 20 minutes. Remove puffs from oven; split and cool.

Filling:

1 package (3½ oz.) sliced smoked beef, finely snipped (1 cup)
⅓ cup finely chopped celery
2 T. prepared horseradish
⅓ cup Girard's all-purpose dressing or sour cream

Combine ingredients in a bowl and chill. Just before serving, spoon filling into the split puffs. May be served cold, or heated in a 400° oven for 7 minutes. Makes 2 dozen.

52

Relish Tree with Winter Dip

1 10-inch styrofoam "tree"
Aluminum foil (or colored foil)
1 head cauliflower
2 bunches radishes
1 large jar green pimento-stuffed olives
1 large can pitted ripe olives

Cover the styrofoam form with foil, securing edges with small straight pins. Wash cauliflower and break into medium-sized rosettes. Wash radishes and snip off leaves. Drain olives. Place vegetables and olives on toothpicks and stick them into the "relish tree" in an attractive pattern. Colorfully different.

Winter Dip

1 cup sour cream
1 package (8 oz.) cream cheese
¼ tsp. salt
½ tsp. celery salt
2 T. Madeira wine
1 T. minced onion
½ tsp. dry dillweed
5 T. chopped pimento

Combine ingredients in a bowl and mix well. Chill in refrigerator for at least 1 hour before serving. Serve with the Relish Tree.

53

Individual Steak and Kidney Pies

2 lbs. round steak, cut in about forty
   1-inch cubes
2 veal kidneys
2 cups beef stock
½ cup flour
6 T. butter
1 cup red wine
¾ lb. fresh mushrooms, sliced
½ cup parsley
1½ cups thinly sliced onions
¼ tsp. black pepper
½ tsp. salt
1 tsp. rosemary
1 tsp. marjoram
1 bay leaf
Pie crust for 9-inch pie
1 egg yolk

Wash kidneys, cut into quarters and remove all fat and gristle. Dredge kidneys and cubed steak with flour. Brown quickly in butter and season with salt and pepper. Put the meat and onion in a large saucepan with the beef stock and wine; add mushrooms and remaining spices. Cover pan and simmer gently for 2 hours, or until the meat is tender. To thicken stock, mix 1 T. flour with 1 T. water and add. Simmer for a few minutes more, then transfer to small individual baking dishes.

Prepare pie crust or use a mix. Roll dough to ¼-inch thickness and cut to fit the tops of the baking dishes. (Be sure to completely cover the contents.) Brush the crust with an egg yolk mixed with 1 T. water. Bake at 400° for 10 minutes, reduce temperature to 350° and bake an additional 20 minutes, or until the crust is golden. Serves 8.

Fresh Spinach Salad
with Green Goddess Dressing

2 bunches fresh spinach
2 T. crumbled cooked bacon (or Bac-o-Bits)

Green Goddess Dressing:

½ cup sour cream
¼ cup Girard's all-purpose dressing
1 clove fresh garlic, minced
1 tsp. Worcestershire sauce
2 T. anchovy paste
3 T. tarragon vinegar
3 T. minced chives
½ tsp dry mustard
½ tsp. salt
Pepper to taste
⅓ cup snipped parsley
¾ cup mayonnaise

Mix ingredients for Green Goddess dressing in a bowl and chill at least 1 hour before serving. Wash spinach thoroughly, tear into bite-sized pieces and place in a large salad bowl. Add bacon, toss and chill. When ready to serve, pour dressing into a bowl and allow guests to serve themselves the amount they desire.

Stuffed
Filet of Sole
with Lobster and
Wine Sauce

8 sole filets
½ lb. small mushrooms, chopped
½ cup chopped cooked lobster
½ cup chopped onion
4 marinated artichoke hearts, chopped
2 slices soft white bread, swirled in blender
  until shredded
3 T. Parmesan cheese
2 T. margarine
½ tsp. salt
⅛ tsp. white pepper
2 cups white wine (Chablis)

In a saucepan, sauté onions and chopped mushrooms in butter. Add lobster. Mix together bread crumbs, cheese, salt and pepper, and add. Place equal amounts of filling on each filet of sole, roll filets, and secure with toothpicks. Place the rolls in a glass dish and cover with white wine. Marinate for 4 hours, or overnight. Transfer to a shallow casserole, and bake in a preheated oven at 350° for 40 minutes, or until the fish flakes. Remove fish from the casserole and discard all but ½ cup of the broth (to use in preparing sauce). Return sole to casserole.

Sauce:

1 package Lawry's White Wine Sauce mix, or
  1 cup medium sauce made with white wine
½ lb. fresh tiny cocktail shrimp
¼ lb. sliced mushroom caps
½ cup liquid from sole casserole

In a small pan, heat white wine sauce and other ingredients, and pour over the fish in the casserole. Serve with lemon wedges. Serves 8.

55

White and Wild Rice Croquettes

1 package (6 oz.) white and wild rice mix
1 cup thick white sauce
1 egg, beaten
Salt and pepper to taste
Flour for dredging
Bread crumbs
Deep fat for frying

Cook rice in 2 cups of water according to package directions, until liquid is absorbed. Heat white sauce in saucepan and add rice and mushrooms. Stir constantly until the mixture thickens and stands away from the sides of the pan. Season with salt and pepper, and spread mixture on a flat, buttered dish to cool. When completely cooled, divide into 8 equal parts and shape into cones. Dip the cones into flour, then egg, and finally bread crumbs. Fry in deep fat at 390° until brown. Serves 8.

French Broccoli Ring

1 package frozen carrot nuggets
½ tsp. dried dillweed
2 T. melted butter
1 T. flour
¾ cup mayonnaise
¼ cup buttermilk
½ cup canned milk
½ tsp. salt
3 eggs
1 package frozen broccoli

Cook carrots according to package directions, set aside (but keep warm). Blend melted butter, flour, mayonnaise, buttermilk, milk and salt in an electric blender. Partially thaw the broccoli, break into small pieces, and place these in an oiled ring mold. Pour blended, uncooked sauce over broccoli. Set the mold in a large baking pan that has half an inch of water in it. Bake at 350° for 45 minutes. Unmold on a serving platter and fill the center with the hot carrot nuggets. Sprinkle the dillweed over the carrots before serving. Serves 8.

Cherry Parfait

2 cans cherry pie filling
1 qt. vanilla ice cream
1 carton dessert whip
1 jar stemmed maraschino cherries

Prepare dessert whip. Place alternate layers of cherry pie filling and ice cream in individual parfait glasses, topping each serving with dessert whip. Freeze. Just before serving, garnish with stemmed red cherries. (You can make this dessert several days ahead of time, but remember to take the parfaits out of the freezer 15 minutes before serving.) Serve a ladyfinger with each parfait (buy them at a bakery, or use the following recipe).

Ladyfingers

3 eggs, separated
⅓ cup confectioner's sugar
⅓ cup all-purpose flour
pinch of salt
½ tsp. vanilla extract
¼ tsp. rum flavoring

Beat egg yolks until pale yellow with an electric mixer, then clean and dry mixer blades. Beat egg whites until they form a softly mounded shape. Add sugar gradually and continue beating until mixture stands in stiff peaks. Fold carefully into the yolks. Sift flour and salt gently over the top and fold in. Add vanilla and rum flavoring. Shape into thin fingers with a spoon or a very wide decorating tube (No. 18) on a cookie sheet topped with waxed paper. Bake in a preheated oven at 350° for 12 minutes. Cool on a cake rack, sprinkle with confectioner's sugar. Makes 18.

Old North Church has been made a legend in poetry, but the building itself is no myth. Even today, surrounded by the skyscrapers of modern Boston, the church's beautiful spire can be seen from many areas. As you enter the small vestibule and then go through the sanctuary doors, it is impossible to believe that this church is 250 years old.

The gleaming brass chandeliers each have 12 candles and a dove of peace. First lighted on Christmas morning of 1724, they are still in use today. (You can tell, because there is sometimes candlewax from evening services on the carpet.) The boxed pews have rather high walls, and each seats five people. Brass plates give the name of the family that owned the pew. Families brought their own foot-warmers, with hot coals inside, because the church was not heated.

The church has plain glass windows and a simple altar. Recessed behind the altar is a painting of the Last Supper, and adjacent panels bear the Ten Commandments, Apostles' Creed and Lord's Prayer. The pulpit, on the left side of the church, is elevated (otherwise, it would be impossible for the congregation to see the minister over the high sides of the pews).

The church's bells were cast in Gloucester, England. Five years after they were installed, Paul Revere was granted a request to form a guild of bell ringers with six of his friends. An organ was built for the church in 1759, and its mellow tones fill the sanctuary today. The clock in the back of the church, built by two members in 1726, still ticks merrily away!

The church was closed for three years during the Revolution, because conflicts between members who wanted Independence and those who did not became so intense that it was impossible to hold religious services. In less troubled times, the church served as a social center. My Old North Church party includes a light supper similar to those served before Wednesday-night prayer meetings. I send invitations a couple of weeks before the party, and plan an evening of gaming— bridge, backgammon, bingo, dominos or whatever games your friends enjoy most.

The beauty of the menu is its simplicity. Everything can be done the day before the party, or in the morning. That way, you can be a calm hostess.

Overleaf. Interior view, Old North Church, Boston, Massachusetts. Officially named Christ Church, this building was constructed between 1723 and 1745, after Boston's population had outgrown its first Anglican church, King's Chapel. The church's architect is not known, although the style is that of the famed British designer Sir Christopher Wren. Officially affiliated with the Episcopal Church ever since the Revolution, Old North Church has also been open to other denominations since colonial times, and ecumenical services are often held there today.

CHAPTER 5

Boston's Old North Church

A Souper Supper

Come to a Souper Supper!

From the bell tower of Old North Church on April 18, 1775, lanterns warned the colonists that British troops were marching to Lexington and Concord. The light from the steeple signaled the beginning of the Revolutionary War.

Come for
Supper and "Parlor Games"

Date:

Time:

Place:

RSVP

MENU

Suggested Wines:

Coffee Table Nibbles

Pedro Domecq Laina

North Church Spinach Salad with Lexington Dressing

New England Clam Chowder

Concannon Vineyard Semillon

Pilot or Oyster Crackers
Hot Fresh Bread

Boston Cream Pie

Hann's Kornell, Brut

Raspberry Torte

Coffee and Tea

Coffee Table Nibbles

Offer mixed nuts, cheese spreads and crackers. Keep the nibbles simple, using only items that can be purchased and served without further preparation.

North Church Spinach Salad

4 bunches fresh spinach
4 green onions, sliced (tops and bottoms)
3 T. crumbled bacon or Baco-o-bits
1 hard-cooked egg, chopped
Cherry tomatoes

Wash spinach carefully and break into bite-sized pieces. Place in a bowl and add onions, bacon and egg. Mix, and top with cherry tomatoes. Pass Lexington Dressing.

Lexington Dressing

1 cup salad oil
½ cup white vinegar
4 T. sugar
1 tsp. salt
1 tsp. dry mustard
½ tsp. white pepper
½ tsp. onion juice
½ cup crumbled blue cheese

Combine ingredients in a jar. Cover and shake. Refrigerate.

New England Clam Chowder

4 T. butter
3 medium onions, minced
4 large white potatoes
4 cans (7 oz. each) minced clams, drained (reserve liquid)
1 can (8 oz.) clam juice
¼ tsp. white pepper
3 cups milk

Melt the butter in a small saucepan, add onions and cook until clear. Meanwhile, peel potatoes and cut into small cubes. When onions are ready, add potatoes and clam juice. Cover pan and simmer until potatoes are tender. Add clams, milk and pepper. Heat—but do not boil. Makes 8 servings.

Boston Cream Pie

⅓ cup butter
1 cup sugar
2 eggs, beaten
2 cups cake flour
2 tsp. baking powder
½ tsp. salt
⅔ cup milk
Cream filling
Chocolate glaze

Cream butter and sugar. Add eggs, and mix well. Sift together flour, baking powder and salt, and add to creamed mixture alternately with milk. Mix well. Pour into two greased and floured 8-inch cake pans, and bake in a preheated 375° oven for 20 minutes. Turn onto a cake rack and cool. Prepare filling and glaze. To assemble, place one of the layers on a serving platter and spread with filling. Place other layer on top. Pour glaze over the cake. Serves 8.

Filling:

⅓ cup sugar
2 T. flour
⅛ tsp. salt
1¼ cup milk
2 eggs yolks, slightly beaten
2 tsp. vanilla

Blend sugar, flour and salt in a medium-sized saucepan. Combine milk and egg yolks, and gradually stir into sugar mixture. Cook over medium heat until it thickens and boils one minute, stirring constantly. Remove from heat and stir in vanilla. Cool.

Chocolate Glaze:

Melt 2 oz. unsweetened chocolate and 3 T. butter over low heat in a small saucepan. Remove from heat and stir in 1 cup confectioner's sugar and 1 tsp. vanilla. Mix in 1 or 2 T. hot water, until glaze is right consistency.

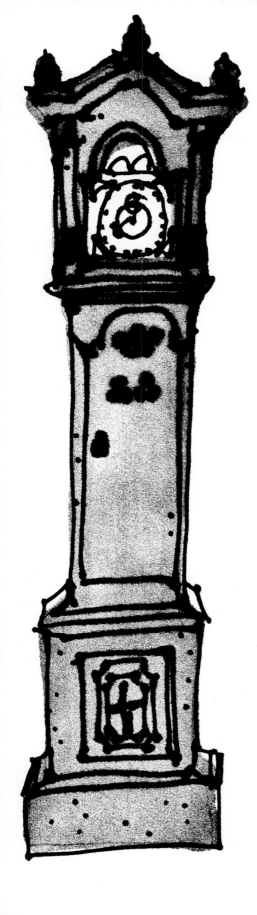

Raspberry Torte

2 packages (10 oz. each) frozen raspberries
1¼ cups sugar
½ cup water
1 tsp. light corn syrup
4 egg whites
2 T. cherry brandy
1 pt. whipping cream
2 doz. ladyfingers

Purée berries and strain (there should be 2 cups). Combine sugar, water and corn syrup. Bring to a boil and cook until syrup reaches soft ball stage (238° on candy thermometer). Beat egg whites until soft peaks form. Gradually beat in hot syrup, continue beating at high speed for 8 minutes, or until meringue cools to room temperature. Fold in the raspberry purée and cherry brandy. Whip cream until stiff and fold in. Line a greased springform pan with ladyfingers. Pour in mixture, cover and freeze for 8 hours or longer. To serve, remove sides of pan and garnish top with berries. This will keep in the freezer for 3 weeks. Makes up to 12 servings.

When the British Parliament was considering stern treatment for the American colonies in 1765, a member who had lived in America spoke out against such a move, saying that the colonists were "sons of liberty." Reports of the speech were sent to America, and embittered colonists soon began to call themselves Sons of Liberty. From southern settlements to those of the north, each had its active group of semi-military, semi-secret Sons of Liberty. An effective means of communication was set up.

All this was achieved at no little risk, for what the men who have become our national heroes were engaging in was treason against the British government, punishable by death. The patriots of Boston designated an elm tree as a meeting place; under the branches of this famous tree, which stands today at the corner of Washington and Essex Streets, messages were exchanged and bulletins were posted. The elm became recognized as a symbol of the revolution, and was used to adorn banners.

In other colonies, Liberty Poles were erected in town squares—a sign that Tories were not welcome. As the oppression of the British government became even more intense, colonists continued to meet secretly—sometimes in the dark of night, sometimes by morning, when they held breakfast meetings.

First course of the day, in those times, was traditionally pancakes. Colonists, both wealthy and poor, were fond of Johnny Cakes. It is said that the first European settlers learned to make them from the Indians, and that the name is derived from "Shawnee Cakes." Another legend says the name comes from "Journey Cakes," since they were commonly carried by travelers. Whichever, the cakes were made of heavy and coarse flour; today, flour is more highly refined and we add eggs.

For this breakfast, I use a cheerful yellow tablecloth, with a miniature "Liberty Tree" as a centerpiece. Guests are greeted with iced Bloody Mary Cocktails—or plain tomato juice, for those who don't care for an alcoholic drink preceding breakfast. The menu is simple, but be sure the food is brought to the table nice and hot.

Overleaf. *Elm tree, Boston, Massachusetts. This blooming elm is representative of similar trees that were held to be symbols of liberty in Revolutionary days. The site of the original Liberty Tree, under which patriots once met, is now marked by a plaque located at the corner of Washington and Essex streets in Boston.*

CHAPTER 6

The Patriots' Meeting

A Johnny Cake Breakfast

FOLD

INFO

CUT
TREE
OUT

Please Come to a Patriots' Breakfast

Sons of Liberty
The Sons of Liberty united to protest taxation without repre-
sentation, which was in force under the Stamp Act. They
carried their cause from a formal protest to the winning of
the Revolutionary War. They often met at breakfast, as we
shall do.

Come for Johnny Cakes

Date:

Time:

Place:

RSVP

MENU

Bloody Mary Cocktails

Fresh Fruit Compote

Fresh Homemade Sausage

Yankee Eggs

Johnny Cakes

Philadelphia Cinnamon Twists

Coffee or Tea

Clockwise from Fresh Fruit Compote (in copper pot): Johnny Cakes, Fresh Homemade Sausage, Yankee Eggs, Hot Coffee, Bloody Mary.

Fresh Homemade Sausage

(Richard Jackson)

2 lbs. ground lean pork
1 tsp. sage
1 tsp. salt
½ tsp. allspice
½ tsp. MSG
½ tsp. cayenne pepper

Select a lean shoulder of pork, or a pork butt roast, and ask the butcher to bone and grind it for you. Add seasonings and mix well. Shape sausage into patties 2–3 inches in diameter and ¼ to ½ inch thick. (Sausage can also be put into casings, using an attachment to a food grinder or a wide plain (No. 7) pastry tip; tie at regular intervals.) Brown sausage over moderate heat, reduce temperature and cook slowly until thoroughly done (15–20 minutes).

Yankee Eggs

2 medium apples, peeled and diced
4 T. chopped pecans
Fat reserved from frying sausage
16 eggs
¼ cup light cream
½ tsp. salt
¼ tsp. pepper
2 T. butter
4 tsp. chopped chives
2 T. minced parsley
¼ cup grated Cheddar cheese

Sauté apples in sausage drippings and when almost done, add the chopped pecans; set aside. Beat eggs until light and frothy, add cream and beat well. Add salt and pepper. Heat butter in frying pan and scramble eggs. Gently add apple-pecan mixture. Garnish with chopped chives and parsley, and sprinkle the top with Cheddar cheese. Serves 8.

Johnny Cakes

1 cup milk
1 cup buttermilk
1 tsp. salt
1 tsp. soda
1 T. melted butter
1 T. sugar
Cornmeal

Mix ingredients together, adding enough cornmeal to make a thick batter. Spread on a buttered baking sheet. Bake at 375° for 40 minutes, or until done. Break apart to eat, or slice into squares. Serves 8. Serve with butter.

Philadelphia Cinnamon Twists

Separate canned refrigerated biscuits, shaping each into a finger-length roll. Coat each roll lightly with melted butter, then dip into a mixture of 3 parts granulated sugar to 1 part cinnamon. Twist rolls, then place on greased baking sheet. Sprinkle with chopped pecans, and let stand 15 minutes. Bake at 400° for 10–12 minutes.

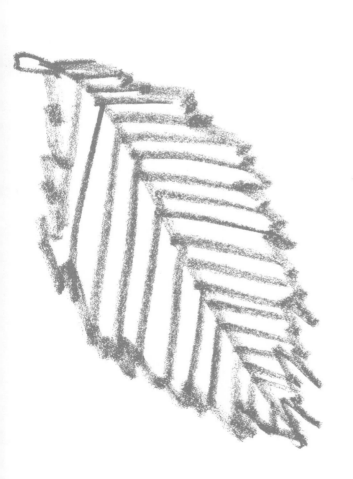

Just before the first shots of the Revolutionary War were fired at Lexington, this poem by an anonymous author appeared in newspapers throughout the American colonies:

No more shall my teacup so generous be
In filling the cups with this pernicious tea;
For I'll fill it with water and drink out the same,
Before I'll lose LIBERTY that dearest name,
Because I am taught (and believe it is fact)
That our ruin is aimed at, in the late act
  of imposing a duty on all foreign teas,
Which detestable stuff we can quit when
  we please!

The furor over tea came about when the British government put a high tax on tea and other products exported to the New England colonies. In 1767, after the colonists started buying tea from Dutch traders, the tax was lowered, but groups of agitated colonists demanded that it be removed completely. Six years later, the British East India Company reached the brink of bankruptcy—and the government offered a substantial tax rebate for tea the company could sell in America. The tea was consigned to individuals who had been given a monopoly for its sale, and it was cheaper than that of the Dutch. The colonists feared that local merchants would be put out of business, and that the British would form monopolies for the sale of additional goods in the colonies.

When the shipload of tea arrived in Boston Harbor, some 7,000 colonists gathered at Old South Church and asked the governor to send it back to England. He refused. A group of patriots disguised as Mohawk Indians then boarded the unguarded ship and dumped the contents of 342 tea chests in the bay. (A tidy crew of marauders, they swept the decks of the ship clean before leaving.)

The British blockaded Boston Harbor for months. In sympathy, people from other colonies stopped drinking imported tea, substituting teas made from sage, rosemary, blackberry and currant leaves. In those days, few hostesses owned teacups—guests invited to tea were expected to bring their own cups, saucers and spoons. The hot tea was customarily poured from the cup into the saucer, and was sipped from the saucer.

Overleaf. *Brigantine* Beaver II, *Boston, Massachusetts. This 110-foot sailing vessel is a full-sized replica of a ship from which angry Revolutionary patriots threw overboard a cargo of tea on December 16, 1773. The* Beaver II *is moored at Griffin's Wharf, site of the original raid. Alongside, on shore, is the Boston Tea Party Museum.*

CHAPTER 7

The Boston Tea Party

An Afternoon Tea

Traditionally, 4 o'clock is tea-time. You may wish to invite guests for another hour that may be more convenient. My dear friend Lea Kates Karp, formerly with the American Tea Council, offers these suggestions for "properly" brewing tea: Bring freshly drawn cold water to a full rolling boil. Meanwhile, preheat the teapot by filling it with hot tap water. When water boils, empty the heating water from the pot and add 1 teaspoon of tea or 1 teabag for each cup. Pour the boiling water over the tea and brew from 3 to 5 minutes. Serve hot with milk, if you want the flavor of the tea to come through, or with lemon if you prefer this flavor to dominate the tea.

I make the sandwiches the day before—or the week before—and freeze them. The lobster canapés are best made in the morning, to be popped under the broiler just before serving. Everything else can be prepared in advance. Do try the Petits Fours—they'll win you many compliments. I use fresh flowers as a centerpiece, surrounding them with attractive trays of food. (And one thing to remember, in planning a tea, is to offer a selection of both sweet and non-sweet foods.)

The historic Boston Tea Party—which was actually not a party but a raid—deserves to be celebrated in high style. So let's have a tea!

Clockwise from tea service: Assorted Mini Sandwiches; Date Nut Bread, Pumpkin Nut Bread, Zucchini Coconut Bread (on tray); Apple Apricot Bread; Petit Pecan Tea Rolls; Lemon Cake Martha Allen (on stand); Petits Fours.

Please Come to a Boston Tea Party

The Boston Tea Party
December 16, 1773
After King George III placed a high tax on tea imported by the American colonies, enraged colonists boarded boats loaded with tea and dumped their contents into Boston Harbor. So it can be said tea started the Revolutionary War.

Date:

Time:

Place:

RSVP

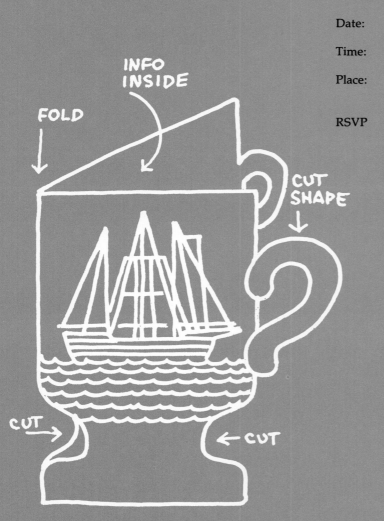

FOLD

INFO INSIDE

CUT SHAPE

CUT

CUT

MENU

Prepare your choice of the following:

Assorted Mini-Sandwiches
Hot Lobster Canapés
Butter Tarts with Mushroom Cream

Celery Stuffed with Pimento Cream Cheese

Zucchini-Coconut Nut Bread
Apple-Apricot Bread
Date-Nut Bread
Pumpkin-Nut Bread
Petit Pecan Tea Rolls

Petits Fours
Waldorf Red Velvet Cake
Lemon Cake

Tea
Champagne Punch
Raspberry Punch
Hawaiian Cup

Assorted Mini-Sandwiches

Use thinly sliced white, whole wheat and rye bread. Trim crusts from the bread with a sharp knife, and spread it lightly with softened butter to prevent its becoming soggy. For a tea, allow 5 mini-sandwiches per person. One cup of filling makes about 5 dozen sandwiches. (If you prepare them ahead and freeze, avoid fillings made with hard-cooked egg whites, raw vegetables and mayonnaise, which do not freeze satisfactorily.)

Setting up a production line speeds up sandwich-making, and it is convenient to prepare fillings a day ahead. When it comes to making the small sandwiches, use your imagination! You can cut different shapes with cookie-cutters, or cut the bread into triangles and small squares. You can make open-face sandwiches, or use two or more layers. Alternating different kinds of bread with variously colored fillings also adds a touch of elegance.

Yellow Cheese Filling:

½ lb. medium-sharp Cheddar cheese
4 strips red pimento, chopped
¼ cup Miracle Whip salad dressing
1 tsp. minced onion

Grate the cheese, add remaining ingredients and blend well. Makes 1½ cups.

Cucumber Filling:

1 container (8 oz.) whipped cream cheese
2 medium-sized cucumbers, grated
4 T. finely minced green onion tops
2 drops green food coloring
Dash of salt

Blend ingredients until smooth.

Chopped Egg Filling:

3 hard-boiled eggs, chopped finely
¼ cup mayonnaise
1 tsp. dried parsley
1 T. chopped onion
½ tsp. prepared mustard
Dash of salt and pepper

Mix ingredients well. Makes 2 cups.

Watercress Filling:

⅓ cup finely chopped watercress (tough stems removed)
3 T. mayonnaise
Dash paprika

Blend ingredients. Makes ¾ cup.

Minced Chicken Filling:

2 chicken breasts, cooked and minced
4 T. mayonnaise
1 T. minced onion
⅛ tsp. paprika
Dash celery salt
Dash white pepper

Blend ingredients to form a paste. Makes 2 cups.

Hot Lobster Canapés

1 can (7½ oz.) lobster
3 T. sherry
¼ cup grated Parmesan cheese
⅓ cup buttered bread crumbs
Paprika

Shred the lobster, add sherry and cheese. Mound mixture on small rounds of bread. Sprinkle with buttered bread crumbs and brown under broiler for just a few minutes. Garnish with paprika. Makes 4 dozen.

Butter Tarts with Mushroom Cream

Tart Shells:

1½ cups flour
⅛ tsp. salt
½ cup butter
1 egg yolk
2–3 T. cold water

Blend flour and salt in a bowl. Cut in butter with pastry blender until pieces are the size of small peas. Mix in the egg yolk with a fork. Add water gradually, mixing lightly until pastry holds together. Shape dough into a ball and chill in refrigerator at least 30 minutes. Remove half of dough from refrigerator and roll about ⅛ inch thick on lightly floured surface. Cut into 3-inch rounds. Gently fit pastry rounds into muffin-pan wells (measuring about 1¾ inches across and 1 inch deep). Flute pastry edges and prick shells thoroughly with a fork. Bake in preheated 375° oven about 15 minutes, or until pastry is lightly browned. Remove tart shells and cool on rack. Repeat with remainder of dough. Makes 24.

Filling:

2 beef bouillon cubes
⅓ cup hot water
½ cup butter
½ lb. mushrooms, chopped
¼ cup minced onion
2 T. flour
1 cup whipping cream, whipped
Watercress

While tart shells are cooling, dissolve bouillon cubes in hot water; set aside to cool. Heat butter in a skillet; add mushrooms and onion. Cook, stirring occasionally, until mushrooms are tender (about 8 minutes). Put flour in a small saucepan and gradually add cooled bouillon, stirring constantly. Continue to stir and bring to boiling; boil 1 minute. Add the mushrooms to this sauce and set aside to cool. When ready to serve, blend whipped cream with mushroom mixture and spoon into tart shells. Garnish with sprigs of watercress.

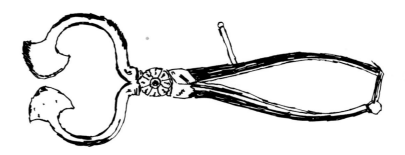

Celery Stuffed
with Pimento Cream Cheese

1 package (8 oz.) cream cheese
1 jar (2 oz.) chopped pimento
⅛ tsp. onion powder
1 tsp. dried parsley
1 tsp. bourbon whiskey
2 bunches celery hearts

Mix all ingredients and fill centers of celery stalks, which have been washed and have had tough strings removed. Cut celery in 2-inch lengths.

Zucchini-Coconut Nut Bread

Wash and grate 3 cups zucchini and set aside. Beat 1 cup salad oil with 2 cups sugar until fluffy. Add 2 slightly beaten eggs and stir until well blended. Mix 3 cups whole-wheat flour, 1 tsp. soda, 1 tsp. salt, 1 tsp. baking powder and 1 tsp. cinnamon. Add this mixture to the salad oil and sugar and blend well. Add 2 tsp. vanilla, 1 cup shredded coconut and the zucchini. Add 1 cup chopped walnuts. Pour mixture into 2 greased and floured loaf pans. Bake in preheated 325° oven 45 minutes to 1 hour, until bread is golden brown and done throughout. Makes 2 loaves.

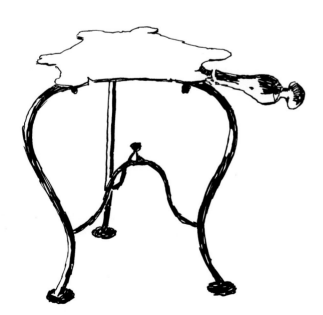

Apple-Apricot Bread

⅔ cup boiling water
1 cup finely diced dried apricots
2 cups sifted flour
2½ tsp. baking powder
¼ tsp. soda
½ tsp. salt
½ tsp. allspice
Milk
½ cup shortening
¾ cup sugar
1 egg, beaten
1 cup finely diced apples
¾ cup chopped walnuts

Pour boiling water over apricots and let stand. Mix and sift flour, baking powder, soda, salt and allspice. Drain apricots, reserving liquid, and pat them dry with a paper towel. Add enough milk to apricot liquid to make ⅔ cup. Cream shortening, adding sugar gradually while continuing to beat. Beat in the egg. Add dry ingredients to creamed mixture alternately with liquid. Combine apples, apricots and walnuts, and fold in. Spoon into a well-greased and floured bread pan and bake in a preheated 350° oven for 1 hour. Turn out of pan and let cool on rack. Makes 1 loaf.

Date-Nut Bread

1 package (8 oz.) dates, chopped
1 cup boiling water
2 T. butter
½ cup sugar
½ cup honey
3 cups sifted all-purpose flour
3 tsp. baking powder
¼ tsp. salt
½ tsp. cinnamon
1 egg, beaten
1 cup chopped walnuts

Combine first 5 ingredients; let cool completely. Sift together flour, baking powder, salt and cinnamon. Add egg to cooled date mixture, then stir this into dry ingredients. Stir in nuts. Bake in well-greased and floured loaf pan (9½x5x3 inches) in preheated 350° oven for 55–65 minutes. Cool before serving.

Pumpkin-Nut Bread

⅓ cup shortening
1 cup brown sugar
2 eggs
1 cup canned pumpkin
¼ cup milk
2 cups sifted all-purpose flour
2 tsp. baking powder
½ tsp. salt
¼ tsp. soda
½ tsp. ginger
¼ tsp. cloves
1 cup broken walnut meats

Cream together shortening and brown sugar until light and fluffy. Add eggs, one at a time, beating well after each addition. Stir in pumpkin and milk. Sift together flour, baking powder, salt, soda and spices, and stir into pumpkin mixture. Beat 1 minute with electric or rotary beater, then stir in nuts. Turn into greased loaf pan (9½x5x3 inches). Bake in preheated 350° oven about 55 minutes, or until done. Remove from pan and cool. Slice and serve with butter or whipped cream cheese.

Petit Pecan Tea Rolls

(Lea Kates Karp)

1 package hot roll mix
¼ cup melted butter (twice)
⅔ cup brown sugar (twice)
4 cups chopped pecans
⅓ cup butter (twice)
⅔ cup brown sugar (twice)

Prepare roll mix according to package directions. Divide into two equal parts, and roll each half on a floured board into an oblong about ¼ inch thick, 8 inches wide and 12 inches long. Spread each half with ¼ cup melted butter, ⅔ cup brown sugar and 1 cup pecans. Roll tightly lengthwise, jelly-roll fashion; seal the edges firmly and cut into 1-inch slices. For each portion, cream together ⅓ cup butter and ⅔ cup brown sugar, spread this in the bottom of a shallow pan or a 10-inch ring mold, and sprinkle with 1 cup pecans. Place the rolls cut-sides down in the pans, with the sides just touching. Cover and let rise until double in bulk (30–60 minutes). Bake in a preheated 375° oven for 20–25 minutes.

Teatime Petits Fours

These are very simple—don't panic! Just read these easy steps, which will make a believer in Petits Fours out of you. They are merely small pieces of cake, cut into different shapes. For the basic cake, bake a white cake (your own or a mix) in a 10x17- or 12x18-inch pan. Cool, then cover and refrigerate for several hours. Cut into dainty shapes, and frost. Decorate with candy flowers, or use a decorating tip to make small flowers of colored frosting. Or sprinkle with candy confections.

Frosting:

¼ cup (½ stick) butter, melted
4 cups powdered sugar
2 T. white corn syrup
¼ cup water
1 tsp. almond flavoring

Combine ingredients in a saucepan and stir until smooth. Heat to lukewarm. (Not hot, please, or it will turn sugary!) Mixture should be like thick cream. Prepare the cake by cutting in bite-sized shapes—squares, rectangles or diamonds. If you want to fill the cakes, put red raspberry or other preserves atop some of them, then top with another cake of the same size and shape. Pour Petits Fours Frosting over the little cakes, and decorate colorfully.

Waldorf Red Velvet Cake

(Martha Allen)

½ cup Crisco
1½ cups sugar
2 eggs
½ tsp. salt
2 T. cocoa
¼ cup red food coloring
1 tsp. vanilla
1 cup buttermilk
2½ cups flour
1 T. vinegar
1 tsp. baking soda

Cream Crisco and sugar. Add eggs and salt, beat 1 minute. Mix cocoa and food coloring to form a paste; add vanilla and buttermilk. Add to egg mixture, alternately with flour. Mix vinegar and baking soda in a cup, and add. (Do not beat, just blend.) Bake in two 9-inch cake pans in preheated 350° oven for 30 minutes. Cool and cut each layer in half horizontally. Frost layers and top.

Frosting:

1 cup milk
5 T. flour
1 cup butter
1 cup powdered sugar
1 tsp. vanilla

Cook milk and flour until thick, and cool in refrigerator. Cream the butter, vanilla and sugar together, using an electric mixer. Slowly add milk and flour mixture, and beat until thick enough to spread.

Lemon Cake

(Martha Allen)

1 package lemon cake mix
1 package lemon Jello
4 eggs
¾ cup salad oil
¾ cup water
½ tsp. lemon extract
½ tsp. almond extract

Combine ingredients and beat until thick. Pour into a greased angel food cake pan and bake in preheated 350° oven for 45 minutes. Remove from pan while hot, prick holes with fork and spoon glaze over the cake.

Glaze:

1 cup powdered sugar
4 T. lemon juice
Grated rind of lemon

Mix ingredients until smooth and spoon over hot cake.

Champagne Punch

1 fifth champagne, chilled
½ cup brandy
½ cup Cointreau
1 bottle (16 oz.) club soda, chilled

Combine ingredients and serve in punch cups. Serves 10.

Raspberry Punch

(Rachael Hill)

4 packages frozen raspberries
1⅓ cup sugar
1 cup pineapple juice
1 qt. orange juice
2 cans frozen lemonade concentrate
2 qts. lemon-lime carbonated beverage

Purée the raspberries in a blender; add sugar, pineapple juice, orange juice and undiluted lemonade. Pour over ice in a punch bowl and add carbonated beverage just before serving. Serves 24.

Hawaiian Cup

(Robert Bowden)

1 qt. pineapple juice
5 fifths champagne
6 oz. brandy
4 oz. Triple Sec liqueur
6 oz. gin

Combine ingredients, adding the champagne last. Add ice to the punch bowl to chill, and serve in punch cups or champagne glasses. Serves 30.

The First Continental Congress was called in September of 1774, in protest against the closing of Boston Harbor and other oppressive steps taken by the British government. The 13 colonies sent 56 delegates to the Congress, and the decisions made at these meetings were the first bricks in the path of America's destiny. After a month of argument and debate, the delegates drew up a "Declaration of Rights." It was agreed that a total trade boycott would be put into effect on December 1—after this date, American colonists would neither import and use any goods from England, nor would they export merchandise to the mother country.

The second session of the Continental Congress convened in May of the following year. Washington appeared in the red-and-blue uniform he had worn in the French and Indian War; he was asked to serve as military leader. Although many of the colonists wished to remain loyal to the king, the word "independence"—in those days a treasonous word—kept coming up in the various proposals. Finally a committee of five delegates was formed to put into proper legal words the group's feelings about Independence.

The historic meetings of the delegates have been described by John Adams in a letter to his wife:

We go to Congress at nine, and there We stay, most earnestly engaged in Debates upon the most abstruse Misteries of State until three in the Afternoon; then We adjourn, and go to Dinner with some of the Nobles of Pennsylvania at four o'clock and feast upon ten thousand Delicacies, and sit drinking Madeira, Claret and Burgundy til six or seven, and then go home, fatigued to deathe with Business, Company and Care . . .

For the Continental Congress party, I make the invitations and my husband sends them to friends who enjoy playing poker. I have the ale running cold from the keg as guests arrive, with frosty chilled mugs waiting for the first guest to "christen" the party. I have arranged the delicatessen items purchased for the party on the buffet table, with bread displayed beautifully in baskets. Garlic Olives and Marinated Mushroom Caps have been made at least a week ahead, the potato salad and Congressional Orange Cake the day before. (Men really go for this cake!)

Overleaf. *Independence Hall, Philadelphia, Pennsylvania. The Second Continental Congress met in 1775 at this hall, which had been built in 1732 as the capitol of the Colony of Pennsylvania. Now the focal point of Independence Hall National Historical Park, it is the most significant structure remaining from the Revolutionary period. Here, George Washington was chosen commander-in-chief of the Continental Army in 1775, the Declaration of Independence was adopted in 1776, and the United States Constitution was drawn up in 1787. Today, Independence Hall stands as the major shrine of the American Revolution.*

The table is set with a dark blue cloth, with a duck decoy—or whatever else I can find that has a "colonial" look—for a centerpiece. Candles flicker from old-fashioned holders. After dinner I clear the table quickly—there is no clutter in the kitchen, as all that needs to be done is put the food away. I stack the dishes for later, and serve dessert and coffee after taking a break. The guests have a relaxed time, and seem to remember the casual poker parties as great fun.

CHAPTER 8

The Continental Congress

Men's Poker Party

Clockwise from Ale Mug: Assorted Breads, Vegetable Platter, Meat and Cheese, Congressional Orange Cake, Favorite Potato Salad. (Delicatessen foods courtesy Michael Dean Gibson, The Sandwich Factory, San Diego, California.)

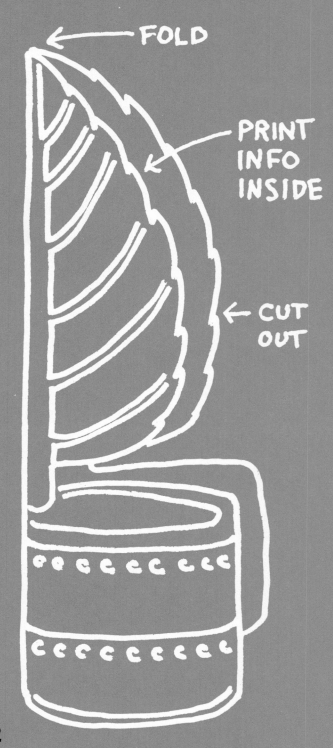

FOLD

PRINT
INFO
INSIDE

CUT
OUT

A Continental Congress Poker Party

Delegates to the first Continental Congress met at Philadelphia on September 5, 1774, to protest the oppressive actions of the British king George III. As a result, our present form of government—Congress and the Presidency—was established. Delegates also agreed upon a "Declaration of Rights": No taxation without representation. We're planning to reactivate the Congress with an all-male poker party.

Date:

Time:

Place:

RSVP

MENU

If wines are desired:

Cold Ale

Assorted Vegetable Platter   Simi Chablis
Garlic Olives
Marinated Mushroom Caps
Sliced Onions and Tomatoes, Shredded Lettuce   Inglenook
Rose Rhine

Assorted Meats and Cheeses

Sesame Rolls, French Rolls, Onion Rolls   Almadén
Zinfandel

Favorite Potato Salad
Kosher Dill Pickles

Congressional Orange Cake

Frosted Fruit Bowl with Strawberries and Grapes   Llords & Elwood
Rosé or Cabernet
or
Jacques Bonet
Coffee   Extra Dry Champagne

Garlic Olives

1 can (8½ oz.) pitted black olives
1 jar (7 oz.) pitted green olives
¼ cup red wine vinegar
½ cup salad oil
1 small onion, sliced in rings
2 cloves garlic, cut into slivers
½ tsp. oregano flakes

Split the olives slightly, using a knife, and place in a jar. Combine remaining ingredients in a bowl and mix well; pour over olives and cover jar tightly. Refrigerate at least 1 week. Drain olives before serving.

Marinated Mushroom Caps

1 lb. fresh small mushrooms
½ cup salad oil
¼ cup white wine vinegar
¼ tsp. salt
1 clove garlic
¼ tsp. oregano
¼ tsp. thyme
¼ tsp. sweet basil
1 T. chopped fresh parsley

Clean the mushroom caps and place in a pan of boiling water for 7 minutes. Drain well. Combine with remaining ingredients, place in a jar and cover tightly. Refrigerate at least 1 week before serving.

Favorite Potato Salad

2 lbs. (about 6 medium-sized) potatoes, unpeeled
1½ cups chopped onions
1 tsp. salt
⅛ tsp. pepper
1 cup salad dressing
1 tsp. prepared mustard
½ cup sliced black olives
8 hard-boiled eggs
Paprika
Parsley sprigs

Boil the unpared potatoes in salted water until tender (30–35 minutes). Drain, cool and peel. Cut potatoes into cubes; combine in large bowl with onion, 6 of the eggs (cut up), mustard and black olives. Season with salt and pepper, and add the salad dressing. Garnish with the remaining eggs, sliced, and sprinkle with paprika and parsley sprigs.

Congressional Orange Cake

1 package (18 oz.) orange or yellow cake mix
1 package (3¾ oz.) vanilla or banana instant
  pudding mix
4 eggs
½ cup cooking oil
¼ cup orange juice
¾ cup Galliano liqueur
2 T. vodka
2 T. Grand Marnier liqueur

Combine cake mix and pudding mix. Add eggs, oil, orange juice, Galliano and vodka; blend in the Grand Marnier. Beat with electric mixer at low speed until blended, then on medium speed for 5 minutes. Pour into a 10-inch bundt pan, which has been greased and floured. Bake in preheated 350° oven for 45 minutes. Cool in pan for 10 minutes, then invert onto serving dish and glaze.

Glaze:

1½ cups sifted powdered sugar
1 T. orange juice
2 T. Galliano liqueur
1 tsp. vodka
1½ tsp. Grand Marnier liqueur

Combine ingredients and drizzle over cake.

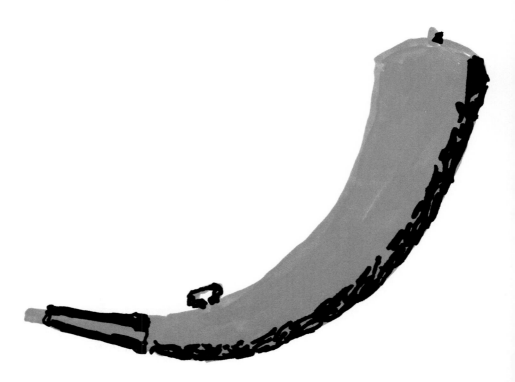

Frosted Fruit

Frost grapes and strawberries (or other small fruits) by dipping them first in lemon juice, then in granulated sugar. They can also be frosted by dipping in slightly beaten egg white before placing in granulated sugar.

The story of Paul Revere's famous ride, as told by the rector of Old North Church, is much more exciting than the version written as poetry by Longfellow. Robert Newman, the church sexton in 1775, is said to have had a friend lock the outside door of the church, while Newman climbed up in the bell tower and signaled with lanterns. When British soldiers banged on the church doors with their gun butts, Newman escaped through a window. He dashed home, put on his nightclothes, jumped into bed, and pretended to have been asleep when the pursuing soldiers arrived at his home. When they accused him of having signaled from the church, he protested that it couldn't have been he, since he'd locked the door himself from the outside earlier that evening and had then returned home. (Fortunately, the soldiers didn't ask to see the key, which his friend still had!)

Paul Revere was one of three people who spread the word, on the fateful night, that the British were coming. Friends rowed Revere across the Charles River, under the cannons of a British gunboat—Revere later said that a full moon was rising, and if the party had been ten minutes later they would have surely been detected.

After Revere and William Dawes, Jr.—another midnight rider—had carried out their orders, they felt their mission would not be complete until they made certain that ammunition and guns hidden around Concord were also safe, so they went on to Concord. (Sympathetic British soldiers had provided the patriots with needed guns and ammunition; unsympathetic British soldiers were engaged in trying to reclaim these for their own army's use.) Revere was captured, and he admitted that the entire countryside had been warned of the arrival of the British troops.

Revere wrote, ". . . the British troops appeared on both sides of the meeting house. In their front was an officer on horseback (Major John Pitcairn). They made a short halt; then I saw and heard a gun fired which appeared to be a pistol. Then I could distinguish two guns, and then a continued roar of musketry. . . ."

Overleaf. *Paul Revere House, Boston, Massachusetts. This residence, nearly a century old when Revere bought it in 1770, is said to be Boston's oldest building. Revere, who lived in the house until 1800, set out from it to give warning of approaching British troops on April 18, 1775. He escaped capture by British officers when they were trapped in a clay pit, but was later overtaken by British soldiers who forced him to admit he had warned the countryside of their arrival. Until immortalized by Henry Wadsworth Longfellow's poem, Revere was known primarily as a silversmith.*

CHAPTER 9

The Midnight Ride of Paul Revere

An After-the-Symphony Dinner

This calm account describes the first shots fired in the American Revolution. The midnight ride leading up to them is a fitting theme for a post-symphony party, and it's an easy way to entertain if you prepare everything in advance. I put all the hot foods in the oven at the lowest setting, and they will hold for hours. (Add the sour cream to the Stroganoff just before serving, however.)

I have a friend serve the cocktails in the living room, while other friends assist me in putting the food in place on the dining room table. Then I relax and enjoy the dinner!

Clockwise from lower right: Brandy Ice Cocktails, Chocolate Mousse, Fluffy Rice, Revere Stroganoff, Lantern Shrimp Salad.

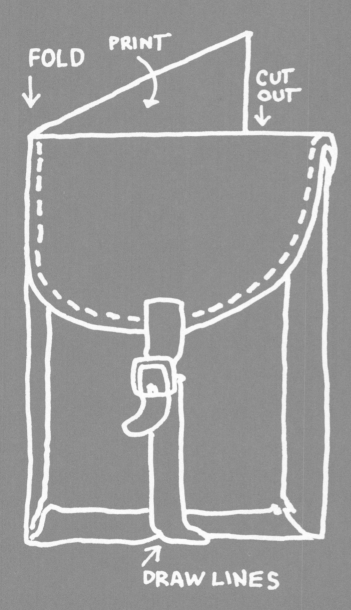

FOLD

PRINT

CUT OUT

DRAW LINES

An After-the-Symphony Dinner

Paul Revere's famous midnight ride, which preceded the first shot fired in the Revolutionary War, is a fitting reason to celebrate an after-the-symphony dinner with us. Do come and help us put a fitting end to an evening of delightful music!

Date:

Time:

Place:

RSVP

MENU

Camembert Delight

Lantern Shrimp Salad

Revere Stroganoff

Fluffy Rice

Parker House Rolls

Chocolate Mousse

Brandy Ice Cocktails

Suggested Wines:

Charles Krug Chenin Blanc
or
Charles Krug Cabernet
Savingona 1965

115

Camembert Delight

Make this the day before your party.

¼ cup cold water
1 envelope unflavored gelatin
2 wedges (1⅓-oz. each) Camembert cheese
¼ lb. blue cheese
1 tsp. Worcestershire sauce
1 egg, separated
½ cup heavy cream, whipped

In glass cup, soften gelatin in cold water; set cup in pan of hot water until gelatin dissolves. Blend cheese together until smooth. Beat in Worcestershire sauce, egg yolk and gelatin. Beat egg white stiff; fold into mousse mixture along with whipped cream. Pour into a 2- or 3-cup mold. Refrigerate overnight. Unmold on serving dish. Serve with rye bread, crackers or rye wafers.

Lantern Shrimp Salad

1 medium cauliflower
¾ cup sliced ripe olives
1 bell pepper, chopped fine
½ lb. cooked small shrimp
½ cup chopped onion
1 cup hearts of Romaine lettuce

Break cauliflower into rosettes and boil in ½ cup water for 5 minutes. Cool and slice. Combine with remaining ingredients and toss, reserving a few shrimp for garnishing.

Dressing:

⅔ cup salad oil
1 T. capers
¼ tsp. tarragon
3 T. lemon juice
¼ cup wine vinegar
½ tsp. salt
1 tsp. sugar
½ tsp. pepper

Blend all ingredients. Pour over vegetables and shrimp. Just before serving line a bowl with lettuce leaves, add the salad and toss well. Serves 4.

Revere Stroganoff

3 lbs. boneless round steak
1 tsp. salt
½ tsp. pepper
Flour
½ lb. (2 cubes) butter
2 large onions, sliced
1 lb. fresh mushrooms, sliced
2 cups water
1 cup red wine
2 cans consomme
1½ cups sour cream, at room temperature

Slice the steak into thin strips 1½-inch long. Salt and pepper the slices and dredge in flour. Heat part of butter in skillet and brown meat slowly. Remove meat, add more butter, and sauté onions until clear and soft. Remove onions, add more butter, and sauté mushrooms until tender. Return meat and onions to skillet, cover with water, wine and consomme. Cover and simmer 2–3 hours, until meat is very tender—add water if necessary. Just before serving, add sour cream. Heat through but do not boil. Serves 8.

Fluffy Rice

3 cups water
4 T. butter
1 tsp. salt
1½ cup converted rice

Bring water, butter and salt to boil. Add rice. Cover, and simmer 25 minutes. Fluff with a fork. Serves 8.

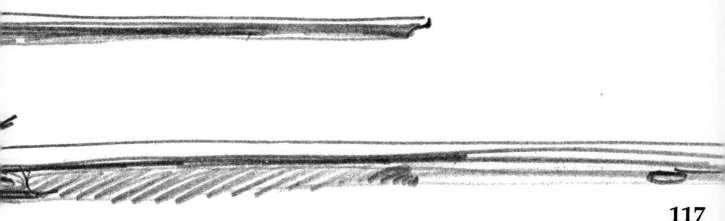

Chocolate Mousse

8 oz. semi-sweet chocolate
2 eggs, separated
¼ cup (½ cube) butter
1 T. water
1 oz. brandy
1½ tsp. instant coffee
3 egg whites
1 pt. whipping cream, whipped

Melt chocolate in double boiler until smooth. Add egg yolks as soon as chocolate is melted, one at a time, mixing well. Melt the butter in the chocolate. Add brandy and coffee. Cool over ice, stirring until thickened but not hard. Beat egg whites stiff. Beat whipped cream separately until it stands in stiff peaks. Carefully mix egg whites and cream together, and fold into chocolate mixture. Be careful not to overmix! Some of the white mixture should still be visible. Serves 8.

Brandy Ice Cocktail

1 oz. brandy
1 oz. Creme de Cacao
2 large scoops English toffee ice cream
10 ice cubes

Place all ingredients in a blender. Frappé until ice is blended and the drink has the consistency of a milk shake. Makes one large cocktail.

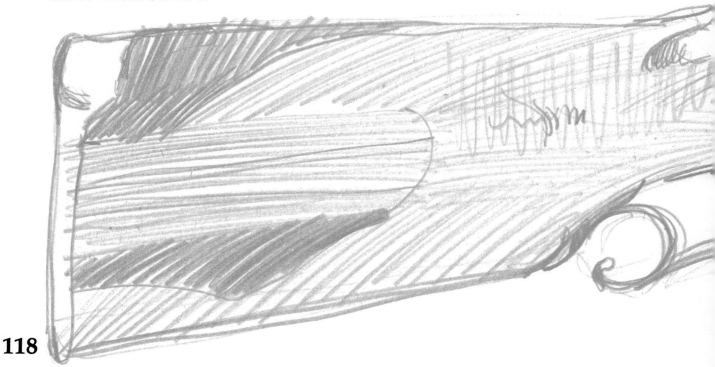

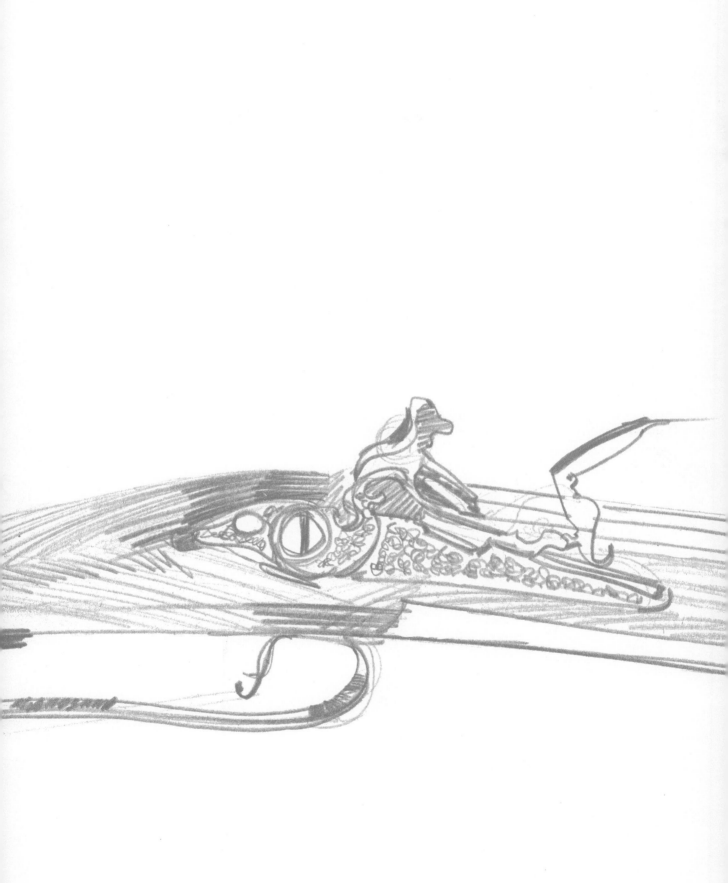

Thomas Jefferson was one of our nation's first Renaissance Men. He loved music, and played the violin with skill. He devised our system of coinage. He designed the state capitol of Virginia, the first buildings of the University of Virginia and his own beautiful home, Monticello. As eldest son, he took over the responsibilities of running the family's 2500-acre estate at the age of 14, when his father died. He had a good knowledge of Latin, Greek, French, Spanish, Italian and Anglo-Saxon. He was skilled in calculus and higher mathematics, and he wrote discerningly about natural history. He served as governor of Virginia, Congressman, Minister to France, Secretary of State, Vice President—and President.

And, in addition, Jefferson was also a connoisseur of fine wines and good food. He hired a French chef to supervise his kitchen, and he introduced pasta, Parmesan cheese, capers, pistachio nuts and anchovies to the United States. Records show that he spent more than $2000 a year on wines imported from France, Italy and Germany.

Jefferson was the first President to live in the White House, where he introduced a new custom—round or oval tables, which avoided the necessity of establishing social positions among the diners, since there was no "head" or "foot." Jefferson liked dinner to begin at 3:30 or 4 in the afternoon—and guests often lingered past midnight.

Jefferson retired to his home at Monticello, which he described, after the death of his wife, as being "big enough for two emperors, one Pope, and the grand Lama."

Overleaf. *West Front, Monticello, Virginia. Unlike other colonial plantation houses, Thomas Jefferson's mansion is situated on a leveled hilltop, some 860 feet above sea level. Completed between 1768 and 1810, it was designed by its owner, who placed the outbuildings unobtrusively on terraces below the main house, connecting them with a sheltered passageway. Monticello is three stories high and has 35 rooms, including 12 in a basement. Some 35 years ago, the gardens were restored in accordance with Jefferson's own plans. Monticello is maintained by the Thomas Jefferson Memorial Foundation, founded in 1923.*

CHAPTER 10

Christmas with Thomas Jefferson

A Tree-Trimming Party with a French Dinner

The menu selected for our Christmas Tree-Trimming party is French, and the French Cultural Attaché in New York has authenticated the fact that all of these foods were eaten in Jefferson's time (although the recipes have been adjusted to modern tastes). This is a most elegant dinner, but even though you can prepare most of it days ahead, it takes considerable time. (Every year, amidst my preparations, it occurs to me that it would be nice to have a resident chef for this particular dinner.)

This dinner is semi-formal—with women guests wearing long dresses. We eat at 6:30 or 7, and return to the living room for dessert, coffee and tree-trimming. The same 12 guests and their children have been invited for the past seven years, and traditions have been established. Everyone has settled comfortably into his or her own tree-trimming niche, by this time, which makes this party one of the most warming of my entertaining year.

From left: Bûche de Noël, Pilau of Rice Pignolia, Filet de Boeuf Wellington, Baked Tomatoes Florentine, Wine.

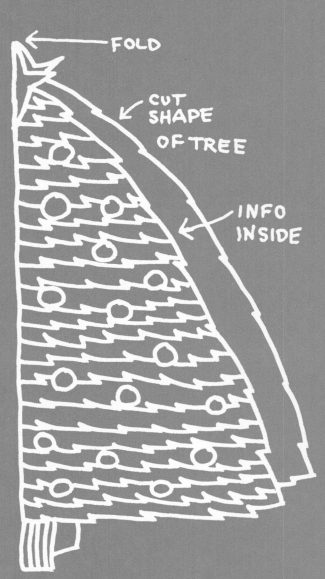

FOLD

CUT
SHAPE
OF TREE

INFO
INSIDE

Please Join Us for Christmas Dinner

1776 Christmas with Thomas Jefferson
This President was the first enthusiast of French cuisine to live
in the White House; he was also fond of fine French wines. Please
come to celebrate with us and share our Jefferson-style dinner—
and afterward, to trim the tree beside our cracking fire.

Date:

Time:

Place:

RSVP

126

MENU

Suggested Wines:

Deviled Egg with Anchovies on Watercress
Pecan Cheese Log with Unsalted English Biscuits
French Shrimp en Coquille

Bâtarde
Montrachet 1970

Soup à l'Oignon Gratinée

Salad Greens with Delicious Roquefort Dressing

Filet de Boeuf Wellington

Chateau Lafite 1961
or
Chateau Margaux 1966

Pilau of Rice Pignolia
Baked Tomatoes Florentine

Fruits and Cheese
Bûche de Noël
Spiced Pears

Chateau d'Yquem
1970–1972

Coffee or Cafe au Lait

Deviled Eggs
with Anchovies on Watercress

1 doz. eggs
Girard's all-purpose dressing
Salt and pepper to taste
Dot of prepared mustard
Anchovy paste
Finely chopped chives
Anchovy strips
Paprika
Watercress

Hard-boil the eggs and place immediately in cold water. Peel and cut in half lengthwise. Remove yolks and place in a mixing bowl, set whites aside. Mash yolks with a fork, moisten with dressing, and add salt, pepper, anchovy paste and mustard. Fill the egg whites with the yolk mixture, using a pastry tube with a star tip. Garnish each egg with a small strip of anchovy, chives and a sprinkle of paprika. Place on a serving tray lined with fresh watercress. Chill before serving.

Pecan Cheese Log
with Unsalted English Biscuits

1 package (8 oz.) cream cheese
1½ cups grated yellow cheese
1 jar (5 oz.) smoke-flavored cheese spread
1½ tsp. Worcestershire sauce
½ tsp. dry mustard
¼ tsp. salt
1 cup chopped pecans

Mix all the ingredients except the pecans, and form the mixture into a log. Roll the log in the chopped pecans and chill at least 4 hours before serving. Serve with unsalted English biscuits.

French Shrimp en Coquille

Boil 1½ lbs. shelled shrimp and drain. In a saucepan, melt ¼ cup butter, stir in 4 T. flour and cook slightly. Add 2 cups nonfat milk, all at once. Cook, stirring, until thickened. Add the shrimp, ¼ cup sherry, ¾ tsp. salt, ⅛ tsp. white pepper and a dash of paprika. Place mixture in eight coquilles, or flat shells (if you don't have these, shallow individual baking dishes will do). Sprinkle with grated Parmesan cheese. Broil 3 to 4 inches from the heat until the cheese browns. Serves 8.

Soup à l'Oignon Gratinée

8 large onions
1 clove garlic, crushed
8 T. butter
1 T. flour
8 cups chicken stock
3 tsp. Maggi seasoning
1 tsp. salt
1 tsp. pepper
6 T. Madeira wine
Oven-dried French bread (allow 2 slices
**   per bowl)**
1 lb. Swiss Gruyere cheese, grated

Slice onions very thin, and sauté with crushed garlic in butter until golden. Sprinkle with flour. Cover with the cold chicken broth; add salt, pepper and Maggi seasoning. Simmer for 1 hour. Add wine. In each individual ovenproof serving bowl, place one slice of bread and sprinkle with 3 T. grated cheese. Pour soup over this (bread will float to the surface). Top with the second slice of bread, then cover top of bowl completely with the remaining cheese. Put under broiler for 2 or 3 minutes, until bubbly; serve piping hot.

Salad Greens

Wash 2 heads iceberg lettuce and drain. Break into bite-sized pieces. Add ½ cup sliced radishes and 4 sliced green onions (tops and bottoms). Toss lightly, being careful not to bruise the lettuce. Place in a plastic bag and store in refrigerator until serving time. When ready to serve, top with Delicious Roquefort Dressing.

Delicious Roquefort Dressing:

1½ cups sour cream
6 oz. Roquefort cheese
3 tsp. lemon juice
¼ cup mayonnaise
¾ cup buttermilk
1 tsp. salt
1 tsp. sugar
1 clove garlic, pressed
2 T. wine vinegar
½ tsp. fresh ground black pepper
Dash cayenne pepper

Combine all ingredients except 3 oz. of the Roquefort cheese in a blender. Blend until smooth and creamy. Crumble the remaining Roquefort and add. Place in a capped glass jar and chill. Makes 2 cups.

Filet de Boeuf Wellington

This famous recipe is fairly complicated—but the work can all be done as much as two days before the dinner, and the raves you will receive make the effort worthwhile. You can trim down the expense by using meat loaf instead of tenderloin—the result is spectacular even with this substitute.

Butter
4½ lbs. beef tenderloin roast
1½ tsp. salt
½ tsp. black seasoned pepper
1 T. clarified butter (see page 173)
½ lb. fresh mushrooms, chopped
2 T. finely minced onion
1 T. finely chopped shallots
2 oz. finely chopped lean ham
¼ cup Serical, Madeira wine
1 large can goose liver paté with truffles
Salt and pepper to taste
2 packages frozen patty shells, thawed

Spread a generous layer of butter over meat and season with salt and pepper. Roast in a preheated 450° oven until rare or medium,

as desired. Allow to cool, then place in refrigerator. (You can do this, and also prepare the mixture that goes under the crust, a day or two before your party.)

To make the savory topping for the meat, first wash and finely chop the mushrooms. Place them in a thin cloth and twist it, to extract moisture. Then sauté the mushrooms in butter with the shallots and onions until they begin to brown; add the ham and Serical. Allow to simmer until the liquid is reduced and the mixture becomes thick. Season to taste with salt and pepper. Refrigerate until you are ready to prepare the meat.

Cover the entire surface of the roast or meat loaf with the paté, then spread the top part of the meat with the mushroom mixture.

Meanwhile, thaw the frozen patty shells and form them into a ball. On a lightly floured bread board, roll the dough ⅛-inch thick into an oblong shape—one large enough to completely enfold the beef. Place meat on pastry and fold puff paste around it, covering it completely and trimming off excess dough. Seal the edges together by pinching tightly with your fingers (put the sealed edge underneath). Roll trimmings and cut into decorative shapes; place these on the dough in an attractive pattern. Brush dough with beaten egg white and place on a baking tray; prick here and there, to allow steam to escape. Bake in a preheated oven at 425° until pastry is browned. Serve with Sauce Madère. (Note: If you prepare this in advance, be sure to take it out of the refrigerator at least 1 hour before baking.) Serves 6–8.

Sauce Madère:

3 T. flour
¼ cup reserved pan drippings from the beef
½ tsp. salt
Pepper
½ cup Serical
2 cups water

Combine flour and pan drippings over low heat in a medium-sized saucepan, stirring constantly. Add Serical gradually, continuing to stir, then add water. Cook until thickened and season to taste.

Pilau of Rice, Pignolia

2 cups converted rice
½ cup (1 stick) butter
4 cups chicken stock or broth
½ tsp. salt
½ cup pine nuts

Sauté the rice in butter until grains no longer cling together, then add boiling stock and salt. Cover and turn heat down to simmer. Simmer 25 minutes—do not remove lid during this time. Uncover, and add pine nuts. Serves 8.

Baked Tomatoes Florentine

2 packages (10 oz. each) frozen chopped
  spinach
3 T. butter
4 T. dehydrated onion soup mix
1 cup sour cream
2 T. yoghurt
8 medium-sized tomatoes
2 hard-boiled egg yolks, sieved

Combine spinach and butter; cook over medium heat until the spinach is thawed. Add onion soup mix, sour cream and yoghurt. Heat, but do not allow to boil. Meanwhile, slice off stem ends of tomatoes and scoop out their centers; rinse and pat dry. Fill with spinach mixture and bake in a preheated 350° oven for 15 to 20 minutes, until tomatoes are cooked and tender. Sprinkle with the sieved egg yolk and serve. (You can prepare the tomatoes the day before cooking. Stuff them and place in refrigerator, covered with plastic wrap. Remove 1 hour before baking.) Serves 8.

Bûche de Noël
(Yule Log)

This is the traditional Christmas cake of France. The recipe is much easier to prepare than it appears to be—and the cake looks fantastic (the cognac-flavored chocolate frosting is always a big hit).

The Cake:

6 eggs, separated
¼ tsp. salt
½ cup sugar
1 tsp. vanilla or almond flavoring, or
   ½ tsp. rum extract
½ cup flour
½ cup powdered sugar

Beat egg whites in a very large bowl with salt until they stand in soft peaks. Add 4 T. sugar, 1 T. at a time; continue beating until the meringue is very stiff. In a separate bowl, beat yolks with remaining sugar and vanilla until fluffy. Gently fold about one-fourth the meringue into the yolks, then pour this mixture into the meringue. Gradually sprinkle the flour over the mixture while gently folding it in. Be extremely careful not to over-mix! Pour into a buttered 11x16-inch jelly roll pan that has been topped with buttered waxed paper (let the paper extend slightly over the sides of pan). Bake in a preheated 400° oven for 10 to 12 minutes, until golden. Remove pan from oven and immediately invert on a dish towel that has been sprinkled with ½ cup powdered sugar. Do *not* remove waxed paper yet. Roll cake tightly up lengthwise in the towel, forming a 16-inch-long roll; allow to cool completely. Then gently unroll, remove waxed paper carefully, and trim off hard edges. Prepare fillings and frosting.

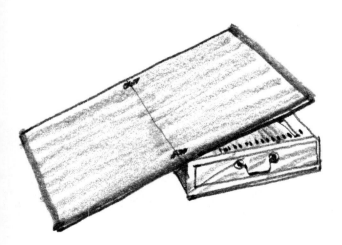

Whipped Cream Filling:

Whip 1 cup whipping cream, combined with 2 T. sugar and ½ tsp. vanilla or rum flavoring.

Mocha Buttercream Filling and Frosting:

1 cup soft butter
⅓ cup shortening
2 tsp. vanilla
⅛ tsp. cream of tartar
3 egg yolks
8 cups powdered sugar
4 T. extra strong coffee
5 oz. melted semi-sweet chocolate
4 T. cognac

Cream butter and shortening together; add vanilla, cream of tartar and egg yolks, and beat until well blended. Add powdered sugar gradually, beating gently until mixture is smooth. Add coffee, chocolate and cognac, and mix until smooth and well-blended.

To Assemble:

Cover unrolled sponge cake with a layer of Mocha Buttercream Filling. Spread this with the whipped cream mixture, then roll the cake up lengthwise. Place seam-side down on serving tray. Cut off the ends of the cake diagonally, about 3 inches in from either end. Trim the ends, placing one on top of the cake and one to the side (use buttercream to hold in place); these form the "branches." Place the buttercream frosting in a large pastry bag with large star tip (a 4B tip is ideal and can be purchased at any J.C. Penney store). Cover the cake with frosting, making long strips and swirls on the ends of the pieces to form cut-off branches. Add a sprig of evergreen (real or artificial) and sprinkle the entire cake with powdered sugar to simulate snow. Chill at least 2 hours before serving.

Spiced Pears

2¼ cups sugar
1 cup cider vinegar
1 T. coriander seed
3 cinnamon sticks (2-inch)
Small piece ginger root
1 whole nutmeg
1 whole clove
3 drops green food coloring
2 lbs. ripe pears, prepared and halved (or 2 cans—1 lb. 13 oz. each—canned pear halves)

In a large enamel saucepan, combine all ingredients except pears. Bring to a boil over low heat and simmer 5 minutes. Using a brush dipped in cold water, wash the crystals from the sides of the pan, so the syrup doesn't turn sugary. Drop pears into syrup a few at a time and simmer 12 minutes or more. (Or until fresh pears are tender.) Place pears in a quart canning jar and pour syrup over the fruit. Refrigerate and serve cold (will keep for 2 months). Serves 8.

In late December of 1776, a battalion of Hessians—German mercenaries hired to fight for the British—was camped on the banks of the Delaware River, in New Jersey. Chunks of ice spun downstream in the chill current. Militarily, the river was impassable. The British were waiting for the river to freeze solid, so troops and cannon could be transported across it.

Across the river on the Pennsylvania bank, General George Washington faced grave problems. The men of his Continental Army were exhausted, ill-clad and half-starved. Many of their enlistments would expire with the coming year—and Washington knew that, tired of losing battles, most would return to their homes. So Washington gambled. He rounded up all the available boats, most of them 60-foot vessels used to transport iron ore and grain on the waterways. On the evening of December 24, with the temperature well below freezing, the army set out on the short but grueling trip across the ice-filled stream. The first boats left the Pennsylvania side at 6 o'clock—the last reached the New Jersey shore at 3 in the morning. Nine miles of road lay ahead, and daylight was not far away. When the American soldiers neared the Hessian bivouac at Trenton, it became obvious that it would be impossible to fire their muskets and rifles, which had been frozen. Washington ordered, ". . . use the bayonet. I am resolved to take Trenton!"

The British, taken by surprise, lost the battle for Trenton, which proved to be the turning point of the war. Congress and the country gained a renewal of courage, and the poorly equipped army was revitalized with new hope.

Overleaf. *Gadby's Tavern, Alexandria, Virginia. This charming tavern was a popular meeting place in colonial times, and its reputation for conviviality served to disguise the fact that some of the people who assembled here were not intent on revelry but on revolution. General George Washington stood on the steps of Gadby's Tavern as the first troops of the Continental Army passed in review. Here he also reviewed the army for the last time.*

CHAPTER 11
Blustery Evening on the Delaware
A Fireside Dinner Party

A fireside party with a Crossing-the-Delaware theme is always welcome in chilly weather. I start the fire early, using a collapsible camping grill and either wood or charcoal. Lighting it a couple of hours before guests are due to arrive ensures that beautifully glowing coals will be waiting for them.

The menu for this party is quite simple, since almost everything is prepared in advance. With all of the work completed ahead of time, you need not knock yourself out on the day of the party. Arriving guests sip Hot Buttered Rum or other beverages, with salmon and cheese straws available on a coffee table. Then, when the cocktail hour is nearly finished, I bring in the steaks and potatoes from the kitchen, nicely arranged on a tray.

Sometimes I pass out slips of paper to each guest during the cocktail hour, and ask them to write their answers to this question: What were the last words George Washington said to his men as they were getting into their boats to cross the Delaware? As the party proceeds, people come up with some fascinating answers! And someone always comes close to the correct one: "Get in the boats, men!" Before the dessert, I present a gift-wrapped prize to the winner. Then, in celebration of the turning point of the Revolution, we flame the Cherries Jubilee and bring the evening to a jubilant close!

Clockwise from top: Cream Horns, Marinated T-Bone Steak, Endive Salad, Fireside French Fries.

**Crossing the Delaware
A Fireside Party**

In late December of 1776, the ill-clad, half-starved Continental Army crossed the Delaware River, led by its brave leader George Washington. Surprised, the mercenary Hessians fighting for the British were defeated. The risky military maneuver and subsequent triumph was the turning point of the Revolutionary War. Won't you join us in honoring this occasion?

Come for Dinner

Date:

Time:

Place:

RSVP

MENU

Smoked Salmon on Picks
Hot Cheese Straws

Marinated T-Bone Steaks

Fireside French Fries

Endive Salad

Herbed French Rolls

Flaming Cherries Jubilee
Cream Horns

Coffee

Suggested Wines:

Charles Krug
Chenin Blanc

Beringer Cabernet Sauvignon
or
Beaulieu Vineyard Cabernet
Sauvignon, Private Reserve

Korbel Natural Champagne

Smoked Salmon on Picks

Cube the smoked salmon (or other smoked fish), and place a colorful frilled cocktail pick in each piece. Arrange artfully on a serving platter.

Hot Cheese Straws

⅓ cup shortening
⅓ cup butter or margarine
1 cup grated Cheddar cheese
1 egg
3 T. water
1⅓ cup sifted all-purpose flour
⅔ cup cornmeal
1 tsp. salt
1 tsp. paprika
Dash cayenne pepper

Beat shortening and butter together until creamy. Stir in cheese, egg and water, blending well. Mix dry ingredients together and add to creamed mixture; blend well. Chill thoroughly, then roll out ⅛-inch thick on lightly floured board or pastry cloth. With a fluted pastry wheel, cut into strips ¾-inch wide and 3 inches long. Place on ungreased cookie sheet. Bake at 375° for about 12 minutes. Cool a few minutes before removing to racks. Makes 4½ dozen.

Marinated T-Bone Steaks

Top sirloin or Porterhouse steaks

Marinade:

2 green onions, sliced (tops and bottoms)
2 cloves garlic, peeled and split
1 cup red Burgundy wine
1 bottle teriyaki sauce
1 T. freshly chopped parsley

Combine ingredients for marinade. Place steaks in a shallow utility dish and marinate overnight, using enough marinade to cover. Barbecue to desired doneness on a grid in fireplace.

Fireside French Fries

Place 2 packages (8 oz. each) frozen French fries in a popcorn popper and toast over coals, shaking occasionally until done (about 15 minutes). Salt to taste.

145

Endive Salad

2 heads endive
2 heads Boston lettuce
1 basket cherry tomatoes
4 green onions, sliced

Wash endive and lettuce and break into bite-sized pieces. Add washed tomatoes and onions. Serve with dressing of your choice. Serves 8.

Herbed French Rolls

½ cup Parmesan cheese
½ lb. butter
2 T. fresh parsley
⅛ tsp. each tarragon and thyme
¼ tsp. garlic powder
¼ tsp. onion flakes
¼ tsp. paprika
French rolls

Combine and blend ingredients except rolls. Split the rolls but don't cut through far enough to separate them completely. Spread the cheese mixture evenly between split rolls. Wrap the rolls in foil and place on fireplace grill until heated through (20 minutes). Watch them carefully, so the cheese doesn't burn.

146

Flaming Cherries Jubilee

1 T. cornstarch
1 T. sugar
1 can (1 lb.) pitted black cherries, drained
  (reserve juice)
2 T. dark rum
1 tsp. grated orange peel
½ tsp. lemon juice
½ cup brandy
Vanilla ice cream

Mix cornstarch and sugar together. Add cherry liquid, rum and orange peel. Cook until thick. Add cherries and lemon juice. Place sauce in chafing dish. Warm the brandy (it won't ignite if it's cold) and spoon into sauce; light sauce. Spoon it flaming over the ice cream, which has been placed in serving dishes. Serves 8.

Cream Horns

2 packages (10 oz. each) frozen patty shells
1 egg white, beaten
Granulated sugar
2 cartons dessert whip
1 tsp. almond extract
(Metal baking cones)

Thaw patty shells and form into one ball. Roll dough out on floured board into a rectangle about 12x18 inches. Trim the edges and cut dough into lengthwise strips about 1-inch wide. Wrap pastry strips around cones, starting at the tip and ending before reaching the bottom; moisten end of dough with a small amount of water, and press to seal in place. Put cones, sealed-side down, on cookie sheet and refrigerate 30 minutes. Bake at 400° for 20 minutes, or until horns are golden brown. Brush with egg white and sprinkle with granulated sugar. Return to oven and bake 5 minutes, to glaze. Cool, and fill with dessert whip to which almond extract has been added. Refrigerate until serving time.

The drawing up of the Declaration of Independence was not a task that proceeded smoothly and without argument. Opinions were divided on what this country's relationship with England should be. Some delegates felt the colonies should try to retain a friendly relationship. Others wanted a complete break.

It was John Adams who offered convincing arguments, which he constantly ended by saying, "A Union and a confederation of thirteen states, independent of Parliament, of Minister and of King!" And those words, of course, constituted treason, so far as the British government was concerned.

Thomas Paine put the case before the people—and gained their support—with his papers (some of which Washington ordered to be read to his troops). Paine's pamphlet *Common Sense,* which was widely distributed, informed the colonists of what the issues were and what their political leaders were thinking.

Finally, a committee was appointed, with the task of preparing a formal statement. Thomas Jefferson, then 33, was chairman and drew up the statement; other members were Benjamin Franklin, John Adams, Roger Sherman and Robert Livingston. Members of the Congress met on July 1 and delegates spoke for or against Independence. The vote taken the next day was in favor of severing ties with England. On the Fourth of July, copies of the committee's formal document were passed out—and, after furious debate, Congress adopted the Declaration of Independence.

Overleaf. *Interior view, Graff House, Philadelphia, Pennsylvania. Thomas Jefferson rented the second-floor rooms of Graff House from May to July of 1776, and in its study he drafted the Declaration of Independence. This study shown here is included in the reconstruction of the house originally built by Jacob Graff, Jr., a Philadelphia bricklayer, in 1775.*

CHAPTER 12

Independence Day

Barbecue in the Park

From the very beginning, July 4 was a national holiday. And the traditional main dish for this celebration, in colonial times, was salmon. Ideally, of course, you would live in a spot where you can catch the salmon fresh that day—as both Washington and Jefferson did. But prepared as in the recipe that follows, fish purchased from a market is almost as good. (Any whole fish, including trout, may be substituted for the salmon.)

We always get together and decide in advance which families will bring what dishes. Then everyone brings food, picnic gear and good cheer, for one of the best parties of the year. By the time we've finished our peanut cream pie, it is nearly time to watch the fireworks display.

So light the sparklers and toast the Declaration with a Blue Coat Lightning!

Clockwise from upper right: Roasted Herbed Corn in Husks, Whole Salmon Stuffed and Grilled, Blue Coat Lightning (in pitcher), Watermelon Basket.

CUT OUT

PRINT INFO

FOLD

DRAW STARS AND STRIPES

An Independence Day Barbecue

Our country's birthday, July 4, is also one of our very oldest national holidays. And it arrives at a wonderful time of year for celebrating. Please come and help us honor the event with a picnic barbecue!

Date:

Time

Place:

RSVP

MENU

Suggested Wines:

Blue Coat Lightning
Planter's Punch
Champagne Julep

Cold Crisp Vegetables—Cherry Tomatoes,
Celery Puffs, Carrot Sticks, Sliced Zucchini

Wente Brothers
Grey Reisling

Whole Salmon, Stuffed and Grilled

Grilled Cheese Potatoes
Roasted Herbed Corn in Husks
Marinated Bean Salad

Tarragon Loaf

Watermelon Basket
Peanut Creamed Pie

Simi Pinot Chardonnay

Coffee

155

Blue Coat Lightning

1 can (6 oz.) frozen limeade
Canful of water
Canful of gin
Ice cubes

Place first 2 ingredients in blender, fill with ice and frappé until ice is crushed and liquid is foamy. This is fabulously refreshing! Serves 6.

Planter's Punch

1½ oz. lemon juice
2 oz. pineapple juice
1 oz. grenadine
2 oz. rum
1 oz. Meyer rum
4 oz. soda
Dash bitters

Mix and serve over ice, with sprig of mint and fresh fruit. Serves 1.

156

Champagne Julep

2 lumps sugar
2 sprigs mint
½ tsp. sugar
2 oz. sweet and sour mix
5 oz. champagne

Muddle all ingredients except champagne, add ice and pour into 10-oz. glass. Add champagne. Garnish with a cherry and a slice of orange. Serves 1.

Whole Salmon, Stuffed and Grilled

Whole salmon
1 potato, sliced unpeeled
1 onion, peeled and sliced
1 lemon, sliced
¼ lb. fresh mushrooms
1 bottle white wine
Tartar sauce
Lemon wedges
(Aluminum foil)

Clean salmon, stuff with uncooked vegetables, and place on 3 layers of foil (large enough to enclose fish). Turn up sides of foil, and pour wine over all. Seal the aluminum pouch around the salmon. Place on the coals until the fish is cooked (about 1½ hours). Serve with tartar sauce and lemon wedges.

Grilled Cheese Potatoes

4 large baking potatoes, peeled
Seasoned salt
Seasoned pepper
1 large onion, chopped
2½ cups cubed American cheese
¾ cup soft butter
(Aluminum foil)

Slice the pared potatoes onto a large piece of doubled foil. Sprinkle with salt and pepper. Top with onion and cheese, and dot with butter. Tightly close the foil. Place on grill and barbecue about 1 hour, or until potatoes are tender, turning several times. Serves 8.

Roasted Herbed Corn in Husks

8 ears fresh corn
Butter
¼ cup parsley
¼ tsp. tarragon

Pull back husks but do not detach from ears of corn; remove silk, and pull husks back over corn. Soak in a pail of water for about 30 minutes. Place corn ears on grill and cook over coals 12–15 minutes, turning frequently. Meantime, combine butter with parsley and tarragon. Brush over roasted ears. (To serve, peel back the husks but leave them attached —they make a great handle.)

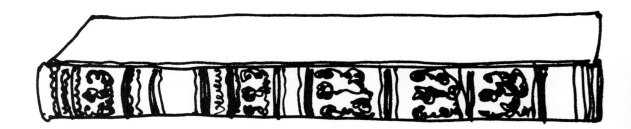

Marinated Bean Salad

(Dorothy Hoersch)

2 cans kidney beans
2 cans garbanzo beans
1 package (10 oz.) frozen peas, thawed
1 cup romaine lettuce hearts, broken in pieces
2 cups cubed Cheddar cheese
¼ cup Italian salad dressing

Combine ingredients and let stand, covered, in refrigerator for 8 hours or overnight. This is great when made the day before. Serves 8.

Tarragon Loaf

Cut two long loaves unsliced sourdough bread in half lengthwise. Spread with softened butter and sprinkle with 2 T. dried tarragon. Place on grill over coals, buttered side down, until toasted. Slice and serve.

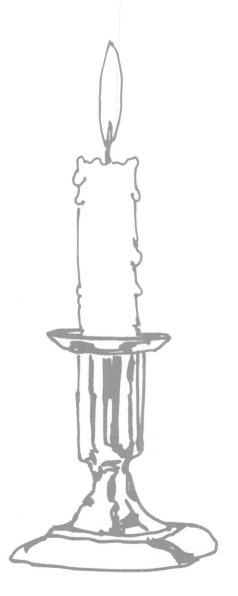

Watermelon Basket

1 watermelon
1 basket strawberries
1 cantaloupe
1 honeydew melon

Remove top third of watermelon and make a basket of the bottom portion, cutting removed fruit into bite-sized pieces. Mix with strawberries and other melons, which have also been cut into small pieces. Fill the basket with the fruit.

Peanut Creamed Pie

⅔ cup sugar
⅓ cup cornstarch
½ tsp. salt
1 can (13 oz.) evaporated milk
1 cup water
3 egg yolks, slightly beaten
1 tsp. vanilla
¼ cup crunchy peanut butter

Combine sugar, cornstarch and salt in medium saucepan; add milk and water. Cook over medium heat until slightly thickened (12–15 minutes), stirring constantly. Do not boil. Add a small amount of this mixture to egg yolks, mix well and return to saucepan. Heat until mixture just begins to boil, stirring constantly. Remove from heat. Stir in vanilla and peanut butter. Pour into baked pastry shell and top with meringue.

Meringue:

3 egg whites
½ tsp. vanilla
¼ tsp. cream of tartar
6 T. sugar
¼ cup salted peanuts, chopped

Beat egg whites (at room temperature) with vanilla and cream of tartar until they form soft peaks. Gradually add sugar and continue beating until stiff and glossy. Place meringue on pie, being sure to bring it all the way to the crust, completely covering filling. Sprinkle with chopped peanuts. Bake at 350° for 12–15 minutes, or until peaks are golden brown.

Betsy Ross, widowed soon after marriage, took over the operations of John Ross' upholstery shop and also gained fame for the flags and pennants she made for ships. She lived a quiet life as a Philadelphia Quaker, eventually married again and bore seven daughters.

In 1870—when preparations were being made for celebration of the nation's Centennial—one of Betsy Ross' grandsons wrote an article in which he said that when he was eleven years old, his grandmother (then 87) had told him the story of how she had made the first flag. Betsy reportedly said that George Washington came to her place of business in June of 1776 accompanied by his friend George Ross (a signer of the Declaration of Independence and an uncle of Betsy's first husband). Ross was a member of the committee appointed to design the flag, and it is said that he and Washington presented Betsy Ross with a rough sketch. According to legend, their design had six-pointed stars, but Betsy insisted that five points would look better—and won.

Overleaf. *Betsy Ross House, Philadelphia, Pennsylvania. This charming little house, located on Arch Street, is unofficially recognized as the residence of the colonial seamstress, although documented proof is lacking. This view shows the kitchen fireplace where Betsy is presumed to have prepared her family's meals.*

CHAPTER 13

Betsy Ross
Sews the Flag

A Needlework Luncheon

Whether the story is true or not, a Betsy Ross party is a good excuse to have a pleasant —and worthwhile—get-together with your friends. I've asked from 8 to 20, at various times. Invitations are sent a couple of weeks ahead; I make the time early—9:30 in the morning—and ask guests to bring whatever arts-and-crafts projects they happen to be working on. It's fun to see what other people are doing, and gives everyone a reason to complete things they'd tucked away unfinished. One year a friend brought with her a piece of needlework, rather raggle-taggle looking, that she'd started five years before when she and I were vacationing together!

I prepare everything in advance, and put the hot dishes in the oven (set at 250°) before the guests arrive. The menu for this party is very simple. The Champagne Punch is superdelicious, and adds a festive touch to a morning get-together. Zuppa Inglese is easy to make but takes a bit of time—it is, of course prepared a day or two ahead. We usually eat between 11:30 and 12:30 and disperse fairly early, since most of us have children to be picked up at school. And the rest of the day goes better, because of a relaxed and pleasant party in the morning.

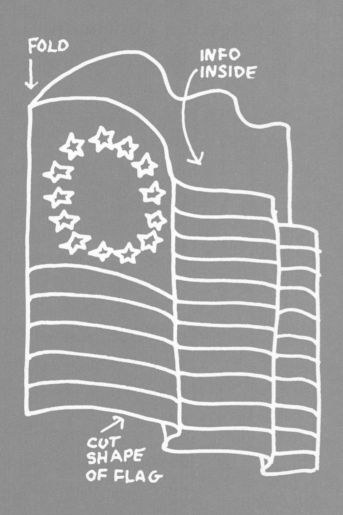

FOLD

INFO INSIDE

CUT SHAPE OF FLAG

A Betsy-Ross-Sews-The Flag Luncheon

Betsy Ross was a well-known seamstress who made flags for ships. Legend says that in 1776 George Washington asked her to make the first flag, and that it was Betsy's idea that the stars have five points instead of six.

Please bring your handwork, and let's have lunch

Date:

Time:

Place:

RSVP

MENU

Suggested Wines:

Fresh Lime Champagne Punch

Hearts of Lettuce with Tarragon Dressing

Crab Quiche Élégant   Graves Ginestet

Buttered Carrots in Colonial Orange Sauce

Zuppa Inglese

Tray of Cheeses: Brie, Comte, Bel Paese   California Ficklin
                                                    Tinta Port

Coffee or Tea

Clockwise from upper right: Hearts of Lettuce Salad, Buttered Carrots and Crab Quiche Elegant (on dinner plate), Crab Quiche Elegant, Zupa Inglese.

Fresh Lime Champagne Punch

2 qts. lemon-lime carbonated soda
1 can (46 oz.) pineapple juice
1 can (46 oz.) orange juice
¾ cup fresh lime juice
2 pints lime sherbet
1 bottle white champagne
Lime slices for garnish

Chill the soda, fruit juices and champagne. Just before serving, combine the juices in a punch bowl. Slowly add the carbonated beverages. Add scoops of sherbet and garnish with floating lime slices. This is really delicious!

Hearts of Lettuce
with Tarragon Dressing

2 heads Boston lettuce
1 T. chopped parsley
1 egg, beaten
1 cup French dressing
1 tsp. MSG
1 T. dried tarragon
2 cans hearts of palm

Wash lettuce and break leaves into a large salad bowl. Toss with hearts of palm, cut into bite-sized chunks. To the French dressing, add remaining ingredients and shake well. Serve dressing over the lettuce and palm.

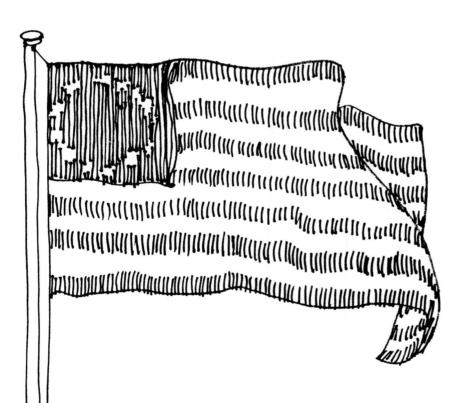

Crab
Quiche Élégant

Prepare this earlier in the morning before the guests arrive. You can make your favorite pie crust or use mine, which is given here. A quiche pan provides a nice touch, but if you don't have one, a 10-inch pie plate is fine.

My favorite pie crust: Place ⅔ cup shortening, 2 cups flour and ¾ tsp. salt in a mixing bowl. Press with a fork until the mixture is flaky; add 6 T. water and mix until it forms a nice ball. Then roll the dough out on a lightly floured pastry board to ⅛-inch thickness. Place in a quiche pan or pie pan, trimming edge.

Filling:

6 oz. Swiss cheese, grated
1½ cups cooked crab meat
2 green onions, sliced (tops and bottoms)
1 tsp. chopped parsley
4 eggs, beaten
1½ cups light cream
¼ tsp. paprika
½ tsp. grated lemon peel
½ tsp. salt
Pepper to taste
½ cup sliced almonds

Sprinkle cheese over the bottom of the pastry-lined pan. Top with the crabmeat, onions and parsley. In a bowl, combine the beaten eggs, cream, paprika, lemon peel and salt; pour this mixture over the crabmeat. Top with almonds. Bake in a preheated oven at 325° for 50 minutes or until set. Let stand for 10 minutes at room temperature before serving. Serves 6.

171

Buttered Carrots
in Colonial Orange Sauce

2 packages (10 oz. each) frozen buttered
   carrot nuggets
3 T. water
2 T. cornstarch
1 T. orange juice
1 T. Curaçao liqueur
2 T. honey
2 T. minced chives
½ tsp. lemon juice

Cook carrots according to package directions.
Set aside but keep hot. Blend cornstarch with
orange juice, honey, Curaçao, water and
lemon juice; cook until thickened, stirring
constantly. Pour this sauce over cooked carrots and sprinkle with chives. Serves 8.

Zuppa
Inglese

This beautiful dessert sounds complicated,
but it's really easy to make—and it is abso-
lutely delectable! Make it one or two days
ahead and keep it in the refrigerator.

6 eggs, separated
1 cup sugar
1½ tsp. vanilla
1 cup sifted flour
½ cup clarified butter, cooled but still liquid
   (see page 173)
1 cup rum

Stir egg yolks and whites separately until
slightly mixed, then combine. Beat until light
and fluffy, adding sugar gradually. Put the
bowl on a rack in a saucepan that has 2 inches
of water in it (don't allow the bowl to touch
the water, however). Place pan over low heat
for 7 minutes, until the egg mixture is just
lukewarm, stirring so it doesn't stick to the
bottom. When mixture becomes a lukewarm
and bright yellow syrup, remove from heat
and beat at high speed with an electric mixer
for 10 to 15 minutes, until it triples in volume
and draws out in ribbon fashion when you
pull a spoon out of it. Sprinkle the flour, a
little at a time, on top of the whipped mixture;
fold in the butter. Bake in a 4½x9-inch loaf
pan at 350° for 25 to 30 minutes. When cool,
divide into 3 layers. Sprinkle layers with rum,
and fill.

To clarify butter:

Melt gently over low heat, carefully pour off clear liquid, discard whey remaining in bottom of pan.

Filling:

3 T. flour
⅛ tsp. salt
⅜ cup sugar
1 cup half-and-half (or cream)
4 egg yolks, beaten
½ tsp. vanilla
½ tsp. almond extract

Mix flour, sugar and salt in a heavy saucepan and gradually blend in the half-and-half or cream. Cook over medium heat, stirring constantly, until the mixture becomes as thick as medium white sauce. Add egg yolks slowly, stirring constantly. Continue to cook until slightly thicker—*but do not boil!* Add the vanilla and almond extracts and blend well. After filling cake, frost or decorate as desired, or top with 1 cup whipping cream, whipped until stiff with 2 T. sugar and ½ tsp. almond or rum flavoring. The number of servings depends on the size of the slices. Sicilian-born Joe Manuel, chef at La Villa restaurant in San Diego, makes a delicious version of this cake, using vanilla, chocolate and strawberry fillings.

Tray of Cheeses

On an attractive tray, arrange your favorite dessert cheeses. It is interesting to offer a varied selection, such as Brie, Comte and Bel Paese.

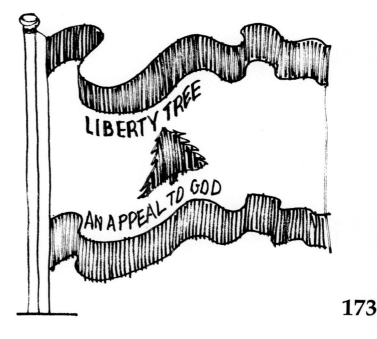

Southwestern Pennsylvania, with its rolling and peaceful landscape, somehow does not seem a fitting setting for a violent conflict that occurred in 1794: the Whiskey Rebellion. Nor did the farmers who raised crops of wheat, corn and rye in this region fit comfortably into the role of rebels against the new nation's government.

It was difficult to transport bulky crops of grain over unpaved, hole-pocked roads to market. Converting the grains to whiskey increased the farmers' profit—and there was a good market for this product in England. But in 1791, the federal government imposed a tax on whiskey, and at that time federal laws also allowed government agents to come into the homes of the farmers as they pleased, to collect the taxes personally from these small producers.

The angry farmers rebelled against what they felt was unfair taxation. Within a year, Congress decided to exempt the smaller distilleries, and the farmers of most states felt the decision eliminated the problem. Not those of Pennsylvania, however. Outraged and determined, they banded together and adamantly refused to pay even the decreased amount of taxes.

Federal marshals were sent to Pennsylvania in 1794 to arrest the leaders of the "whiskey ring." Many small but bitter battles resulted, in which several farmers were killed. Finally, President Washington sent 15,000 troops to the region to put down the handful of rebellious farmers, and Washington himself reviewed the troops at Bedford Springs. This effort to enforce a law passed by the Congress brought him great personal disfavor in Pennsylvania. Eventually, he pardoned two of the rebel leaders who had been placed under arrest. When the released men returned home, their appearance was the cause of much rejoicing and many parties.

Overleaf. *Robertson's Windmill, Williamsburg, Virginia. In the early days of the colonial period, the most popular alcoholic drink was rum, distilled in New England from molasses imported from Caribbean islands. The production of whiskey began in the late 1700s, after colonists from Scotland had settled in western Pennsylvania. The grinding of grains—for use either in making whiskey or making breads— demanded power, and where water power was not available, grinding stones were sometimes driven by windmills similar to the one pictured here.*

CHAPTER 14

The Whiskey Rebellion

An Evening Cocktail Party

The Whiskey Rebellion is every bit as good a reason for a party now as it was then. Invite as many guests as you like—I've had as many as 75. The invitations look like a bottle, and it's entirely appropriate to make this a BYOB party. I also ask people to come dressed as farmers. Some time during the evening, I pass out pieces of paper and ask guests to vote for the couple they think has the best costume. (The winners are presented with a wooden rake tied with a big red-white-and-blue bow.)

Shelling the nuts is a chore (I've done as many as 15 lbs., when there are many guests), but the wonderful aroma that fills the room when they are toasted over coals in the fireplace makes the effort worthwhile. (Lacking a fireplace, you can do them in a skillet.)

The table is set with a red tablecloth, topped with a bouquet of white daisies and old-fashioned candlesticks, which hold lighted blue candles. And it's off to join the rebels!

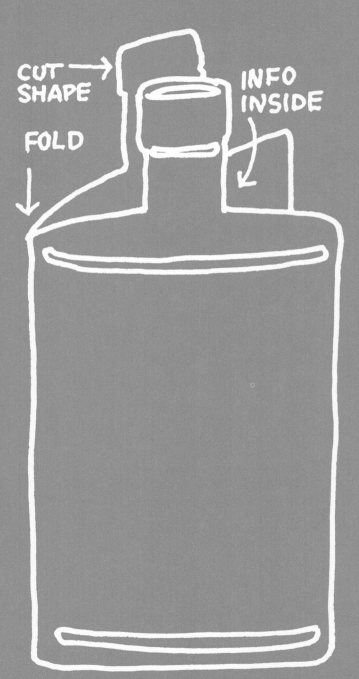

CUT SHAPE →

INFO INSIDE

FOLD

A Whiskey Rebellion Party

In 1794, farmers of southwestern Pennsylvania protested the government's tax on the whiskey they distilled from crops of corn and rye. Although they put up a great fight, they had no chance against President Washington's 15,000 troops. Farmers of the Bedford Springs area really won, though, because Washington lifted the tax and pardoned prisoners the troops had taken.

Won't you please join us for a party (BYOB)?

Date:

Time:

Place:

RSVP

P.S. A prize to the best-dressed farmer couple!

MENU

Dean's Whiskey Reb

Roasted Walnuts
Fried Shrimp with Spicey Cranberry Dip
Farmer Filled Mushroom Caps
Bedford Springs Meat Balls
Pennsylvania Ham Cornucopias
Chilled Colossal Ripe Olives
Sherry Cheddar Walnut Ball with English Biscuits

Party Whiskey Balls

Clockwise from lower left: Fried Shrimp, Pennsylvania Ham Cornucopias, Bedford Shrimp, Meat Balls, Spicey Cranberry Dip, Dean's Whiskey Reb (in glasses), Sherry Cheddar Walnut Balls with English Biscuits, Pecan Whiskey Balls.

Dean's Whiskey Reb

Fill an 8-oz. old-fashioned glass with ice cubes. Pour 2 oz. Scotch whiskey over the ice, and fill the glass with bitter lemon soda. Garnish with a slice of lemon in which an American flag cocktail pick has been placed.

Roasted Walnuts

(Hazel Huntley Jones)

Carefully shell 2 lbs. walnuts. (Broken pieces will do, but halves are much more attractive.) In a 10-inch skillet, melt 4 T. butter over medium heat. Place walnuts in butter and sauté, shaking the skillet continually, until the walnuts are slightly darker in color and are heated through. (Be careful—these burn easily!) Serve in an attractive dish with a miniature silver spoon.

Fried Shrimp
with Spicey Cranberry Dip

1 can (1 lb.) whole-berry cranberry sauce
½ cup chili sauce
2 tsp. prepared horseradish
1 T. fresh lemon juice
1 tsp. dry mustard
1 package (2 lb.) frozen breaded shrimp, fried

In a saucepan, combine all ingredients other than shrimp. Heat mixture to boiling, while stirring constantly. Serve hot as a dip for the fried shrimp. Makes 2 cups.

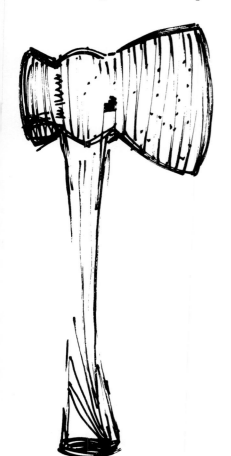

Farmer Filled Mushroom Caps

2 lbs. small whole fresh mushrooms
½ cup butter
2 cups ground ham
½ cup yoghurt
¼ cup Girard's all-purpose dressing
¼ cup sour cream
6 T. minced green onion tops

Wash mushrooms and pat dry with paper towels. Remove the stems and chop these finely. Sauté the caps lightly in the butter, then arrange them in a 9x11-inch glass baking dish. Mix the ground ham, yoghurt, all-purpose dressing, sour cream, onion tops and chopped mushroom stems. Place this mixture on the mushroom caps. Bake in a preheated oven at 350° for about 10 minutes, or until heated through. Garnish with parsley sprigs. Makes 6 dozen.

Pennsylvania Ham Cornucopias

16 slices boiled ham
1 can Cheddar cheese spread
1 can pineapple chunks

Cut the sliced ham diagonally to form triangles. Roll half the triangles into cornucopias, securing them with toothpicks, and fill with the Cheddar cheese spread. Wrap the rest of the triangles around chunks of pineapple, forming cornucopias, and secure with toothpicks. (Make these in the morning, before your party.)

Bedford Springs Meat Balls

2 lbs. lean ground beef
1 package Lipton's dehydrated onion soup mix
1 T. catsup
1 T. chili powder
2 eggs
2 drops Tabasco sauce
3 slices bread, crumbed ⟩ 3/4 c. crushed seasoned croutons
½ tsp. seasoned salt
¼ tsp. poultry seasoning
⅛ tsp. pepper
¼ tsp. celery salt
1 cup catsup 1 cup chili sauce
1 cup grape jelly

Combine all except last two ingredients in a large bowl and mix well. Form into tiny balls the size of an olive. Place the meatballs in a large, shallow glass baking dish, and bake in a preheated oven at 375° for 30 minutes, until they are well browned. During the baking time, turn the meatballs several times so they will cook evenly. Makes 100 meatballs.

For the sauce, combine the 1 cup catsup and the grape jelly and heat thoroughly. Place meatballs in a chafing dish and pour the sauce over them. Serve hot.

Sherry Cheddar Walnut Ball

1 package (8 oz.) cream cheese
1½ cups grated Cheddar cheese
1 T. sherry
1 jar (5 oz.) English flavored cheese spread
½ tsp. dry mustard
½ tsp. salt
1 can (7½ oz.) chopped ripe olives
¼ cup chopped parsley
1 cup chopped walnuts

Mix all ingredients except walnuts and parsley, and form into a ball. Combine walnuts and parsley, and roll the ball in this mixture. Chill at least 4 hours. (This can be made as many as 3 days ahead and kept refrigerated.) Serve chilled with English biscuits (these can be purchased at any grocery store).

Party Whiskey Balls

2¾ cups vanilla wafer crumbs
2 cups confectioner's sugar
1¼ cup finely chopped pecans
2 T. cocoa
2 T. white corn syrup
¼ cup bourbon whiskey

Reserve 1 cup confectioner's sugar. Combine remaining ingredients and mix well. Shape into 1-inch balls and roll them in the reserved sugar. Place in a tightly covered container for at least 1 day before serving (they will keep for as long as 5 weeks). Makes 36 balls.

The mansion at Mount Vernon crowns a hilltop covered by trees, overlooking a sweeping view of the Potomac and the hills of Maryland. In Washington's day, Mount Vernon was a self-contained estate. Around a hundred slaves lived on the main plantation. Ten women worked continuously at spinning fabrics of wool, linen and cotton; they also knit all the socks and sweaters. The wool and cotton, were, of course, raised on the farm. The shoemaker made 217 pairs of shoes in a year and repaired some 120 pairs.

The house was surrounded by stands of flowering trees, bowling greens, and flower gardens enclosed in boxwood hedges. The two-and-a-half-story home, with its tall columns and broad piazza, was—and is—truly elegant. There were so many guests that George Washington once described Mount Vernon as a "well resorted tavern." He and Martha earned reputations as gracious hosts with the impressive meals they served in the beautiful banquet room. In addition to French cuisine, their meals featured native maple sugar, pecans, Virginia ham, biscuits, bacon, eggs, fried apples and hot breads.

Washington was fond of mutton, shad, shrimp and oysters, and liked Johnny cakes and honey for breakfast. He always had a cup of beer for dinner and is said to have drunk many glasses of wine after his meal.

In serving his country, Washington sacrificed personal wealth. He helped support the struggling Continental Army, was generous in giving to the poor, and put most of the profits from his plantation back into this estate. The profits of Mount Vernon were limited additionally by poor soil and slipshod overseers.

Overleaf. *Mount Vernon, Virginia. Originally called Ferry Farm, Mount Vernon was a self-sustaining 40,000-acre plantation in George Washington's time. Today, Mount Vernon encompasses nearly 500 acres. The restored outbuildings surrounding the plantation mansion include a greenhouse, icehouse, spinning house, office, kitchen, smokehouse, laundry and storehouses, as well as quarters that once housed overseers and slaves.*

CHAPTER 15

Southern Plantation Comfort

A Formal Dinner Party

Martha helped the cause of the Revolution far more than was required of her position. She sometimes visited her husband in the lines of battle, brought him food and cooked for the troops. It must have been a pleasant relief for her to return to more gracious circumstances, with the end of the war.

The menu for this party exemplifies the major dishes of the southern plantation. These days, though, we lack the vast armies of kitchen help available in the past. So the recipes have been planned to allow for cooking ahead. This is another occasion when I use my best silver and china. Sometimes I ask my friends to wear long dresses and become—for an evening—Colonial Belles. But on with the party!

Please Try Our Southern Plantation Comfort

Southern hospitality attained its highest point at Mount Vernon, Virginia, with George and Martha Washington as host and hostess. Sample colonial dinner fare with us!

Date:

Time:

Place:

Black Tie or
Colonial Formal

FOLD

INFO

CUT OUT SHAPES

190

MENU

Mint Julep
Ten-Day Mint Julep
Sazerac Cocktail

Oysters Rockefeller
Jambalaya
Corn Sticks
Chicken Gumbo Filé

Deep South Salad
Tournedos Rossini

Potatoes Savannah
Asparagus Sauté

Plantation Biscuits

Rum Cream Pie
Southern Charlotte Russe
Creole Pralines

Hickory Coffee

Suggested Wines:

Wente Brothers Chablis
or
Meursault Louis Jadot

Latour Chateau Iotour 1964
or
Chateau Mouton Rothschild 1966

Moët & Chandon Dom Pérignon
or
Taittinger Blanc de Blanc 1964

Front to back: Asparagus Sauté with Hollandaise Sauce, Tournedos Rossini, Jambalaya, Plantation Biscuits. (Photographed in the home of Mr. and Mrs. Ralph Pesqueira, Jr. Antiques from the private collection of Mr. and Mrs. Robert Abercrombie Padgett.)

Mint Julep

2½ oz. bourbon whiskey
1 tsp. granulated sugar
½ tsp. water
Sprigs of fresh mint

Fill 12- or 14-oz. Collins glass, silver mug or pewter cup with finely cracked ice and pour in whiskey. Dissolve sugar in water (use a little more water if necessary) and add. Agitate the liquid with a bar spoon until glass is frosted. Garnish with a generous sprig of mint, an orange slice and a green cherry. Serve this with a short straw, so your guests can appreciate the bouquet of the drink.

Ten-Day Mint Julep

½ cup sugar
2 jiggers brandy
Bourbon whiskey
Fresh mint sprigs, crushed

Pour sugar into quart jar with lid. Pack jar tightly with sprigs of crushed mint. Add brandy, then fill with bourbon. Do not stir. Screw lid on tightly and refrigerate, inverting jar each day for 10 days. To serve, pour 2 oz. of this concentrate over crushed ice, and garnish with mint sprig. Makes 1 quart.

Sazerac Cocktail

Ice
1 sugar cube
1 tsp. water
Dash Angostura bitters
2 dashes Peychaud bitters
1¼ oz. straight rye whiskey
4 dashes absinthe
Lemon twist

To prepare this drink, you will need two old-fashioned glasses. Fill one of them with ice and set aside. In the other, crush sugar cube in water, then add bitters, rye, ice cubes and stir. Empty ice from first glass, dash in the absinthe, twirl to coat the inside of glass thoroughly, and pour out absinthe. Pour whiskey mixture in this glass and add lemon twist. Serve without ice.

Oysters Rockefeller

1 tsp. anise seed
1 cup water
1 cup oyster juice
1 cup tightly packed fresh parsley leaves
2 cups tightly packed spinach leaves
10 shallots
1 tsp. celery salt
6 drops hot pepper sauce
1 tsp. ground thyme
2 T. anchovy paste
1 lb. bacon strips, finely chopped
2 cloves garlic
1 cup butter
2 tsp. lemon juice
1 cup toasted bread crumbs
4 dozen oysters in shell

Simmer the anise seed in water and oyster juice for 15 minutes; strain seeds from liquid and discard them. Finely chop the parsley, spinach and shallots and simmer them, covered, in the anise liquid for 10 minutes. Add celery salt, pepper sauce, thyme and anchovy paste. Meantime, fry the bacon, add garlic, and cook until nearly brown; add the cooked vegetable mixture. Add butter, lemon juice and bread crumbs. Open oysters and place on the half shell, put shells on a bed of rock salt on a baking sheet. Bake in a preheated 350° oven for about 6 minutes, or until edges of oysters just curl. Remove from oven and spread each oyster with some of the prepared sauce; return to broiler for 5 minutes. Serves 8.

Jambalaya

2 onions, minced
6 T. butter
1 can tomatoes
½ can tomato paste
3 cloves garlic, chopped
2 celery stalks, chopped
½ green bell pepper, chopped
1 tsp. chopped parsley
½ tsp. thyme
3 whole cloves, crumbled
1 cup diced cooked ham
1½ lb. shrimp, cleaned and boiled
3 cups cooked rice
Salt, pepper, cayenne

Sauté onions in butter until clear (about 5 minutes). Add tomatoes and tomato paste, and cook 5 minutes, stirring constantly. Add garlic, celery, bell pepper, parsley, thyme and cloves. Cook 30 minutes, stirring frequently. Add ham and cook 5 minutes. Add shrimp and cook 5 minutes. Stir in rice, season to taste, and simmer 30 minutes. Serves 8.

Corn Sticks

1 cup milk
2 eggs, beaten
1 cup cornmeal
1 cup sifted flour
¾ tsp. salt
2½ tsp. baking powder
1 T. melted butter

Combine milk and eggs, add to sifted dry ingredients. Add butter, and stir to blend. Place in greased corn-stick pan. Bake at 400° for 20 minutes.

Chicken Gumbo Filé

One 4-lb. chicken, cut up
5 cups water
3 chicken bouillon cubes
1 clove garlic
1 T. salt
¼ tsp. pepper
1 sweet red pepper, coarsely chopped
1½ cups chopped onion
3 T. cornstarch
¼ lb. salt pork, diced
2 cups stewed tomatoes
1 package (10 oz.) frozen okra
2 drops hot pepper sauce
2 tsp. gumbo filé powder
Hot cooked rice

Cook the chicken in water, with the bouillon cubes, garlic, salt and pepper, for 3 hours or until tender. Cool. Remove meat from bones and cut into bite-sized pieces. Strain the broth and add enough water to make 6 cups. When cool, skim off the fat, heat it, and sauté red pepper and onion in it for 5 minutes. Add cornstarch, and brown. Gradually stir in broth. Add salt pork and tomatoes. Cover and simmer for 30 minutes. Add chicken and okra. Simmer covered for 10 minutes. Season with salt, pepper and hot pepper sauce. Gradually add filé powder and stir until completely blended (do not boil after adding filé). Put a scoop of rice in the center of each soup bowl, and fill bowl with gumbo. Serves 8.

Deep South Salad

1 head iceberg lettuce
1 head romaine
Chicory
1 lb. bacon, fried crisp and crumbled
4 hard-boiled eggs, coarsely chopped
2 avocados, diced

Fill the bottom of a salad bowl with lettuce, romaine and chicory. Mix in the bacon, eggs and avocados. Serve with following dressing.

Dressing:

1 cup olive oil
½ cup wine vinegar
1 tsp. dry mustard
Salt, black and white pepper

Mix ingredients in a jar, and shake well to blend. Pour a little dressing over the salad; pour the rest over just before serving. Season and toss lightly. Serves 8.

Tournedos Rossini

½ cup (1 stick) butter
3 T. flour
2 cups beef stock
½ tsp. freshly ground pepper
1 bay leaf
⅛ tsp. garlic salt
1 allspice
1 clove
4 T. brandy
4 T. Burgundy
4 T. oil
1 T. tomato paste
8 pieces filet mignon
5 bread rounds, toasted
1 can (1 lb.) pork-liver paté
1 truffle (⅞ oz. can), sliced

Melt butter, blend in flour, and brown. Blend in beef stock, stirring until smooth. Add pepper, bay leaf, garlic salt, allspice and clove; set aside. Heat brandy, Burgundy, oil and tomato paste for sauce.

Broil filets to taste, and place on bread round on serving plate. Put a slice of paté on each filet; garnish with slices of truffle. Pour the hot sauce over all. Serves 8.

Potatoes Savannah

3 cups half-and-half
6 eggs, beaten
½ tsp. salt
¼ tsp. onion powder
⅛ tsp. white pepper
¼ cup parsley
1½ lbs. raw potatoes, sliced
½ cup grated Cheddar cheese

Combine cream and eggs, and season with salt, pepper, onion powder and parsley. Lay sliced potatoes in a casserole. Pour cream mixture over potatoes and top with cheese. Bake at 300°—covered for 30 minutes, uncovered for 15 minutes (or until potatoes become tender). Serves 8.

Asparagus Sauté

1 lb. fresh asparagus
4 T. butter
1 pt. hollandaise sauce
¼ cup slivered almonds

Peel asparagus stems with potato peeler and cut into 1-inch pieces. Sauté until just tender in butter. Do not overcook—asparagus should be slightly crunchy. Top with hollandaise sauce and garnish with slivered almonds. Serves 8.

Simple Hollandaise:

To ½ cup salad dressing or mayonnaise, add 2 tsp. prepared mustard and 1½ tsp. lemon juice. Heat and stir over low heat until hot through—but don't boil.

Plantation Biscuits

2 cups flour
1 T. baking powder
½ tsp. sugar
1 tsp. salt
⅓ cup Crisco
⅔ cup milk

Sift the dry ingredients into a mixing bowl. Cut shortening into flour mixture with a pastry blender. Stir in almost all of the milk—using enough to make a soft and puffy dough that will be easy to roll out. Knead dough a few times, but do not handle too much or it will become tough. Roll out ½-inch thick and cut with 2-inch biscuit cutter. Place on ungreased baking sheet, touching each other. Bake at 450° for 12 minutes. Makes 20.

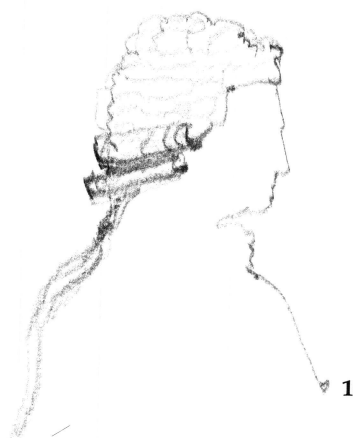

Rum Cream Pie

1 envelope unflavored gelatin
½ cup cold water
5 egg yolks
1 cup sugar
⅓ cup dark rum
1 tsp. vanilla
1½ cup whipping cream
Crumb crust
Chocolate curls

Soften gelatin in cold water. Place over low heat and bring almost to a boil, stirring to dissolve. Beat egg yolks and sugar until very light. Stir gelatin into egg mixture; cool. Gradually add rum and vanilla, beating constantly. Whip the cream until it stands in soft peaks, and fold it into gelatin mixture. Cool until mixture begins to set, then spoon into crumb crust. Chill. Top with chocolate curls for garnish.

Crumb crust:

2½ cups graham cracker crumbs
½ cup butter, melted
2 T. sugar
¼ tsp. cinnamon
⅛ tsp. nut meats, finely chopped

Combine ingredients and press into a 9-inch pie pan. Chill before filling.

Southern Charlotte Russe

About 12 ladyfingers, split
2 envelopes unflavored gelatin
½ cup cold water
4 large egg yolks, beaten slightly
¾ cup sugar
⅛ tsp. salt
2 cups milk
1 tsp. vanilla
¼ cup less 1 tsp. bourbon, rum or sherry
2 cups heavy cream, whipped
Garnishes

Line bottom and sides of an oiled 2½-quart mold or a 7-inch spring-form pan with ladyfingers; set aside. Soften gelatin in cold water and set aside. Combine egg yolks, sugar, salt and ¼ cup milk in top of double boiler. Heat remaining milk and gradually add to egg-yolk mixture. Cook, stirring, over hot water (do not boil) until custard coats a metal spoon. Remove from heat and stir in gelatin and vanilla. Cool over ice water until mixture begins to thicken, then fold in whipped cream. Pour into prepared mold. Chill until ready to serve. Unmold on a pretty silver or crystal serving plate. Garnish as desired with additional whipped cream put through a pastry tube, and top with cherries, berries or other soft fruit in season. Or serve with apricots or peaches canned in heavy syrup. Makes about 10 servings.

Creole Pralines

4 cups sugar
1 cup half-and-half
2 tsp. vanilla
2½ cups chopped pecans
2 T. butter
Dash of salt

Boil 3 cups sugar with half-and-half in a large saucepan until it forms a soft ball (236° on candy thermometer). Meanwhile, melt remaining sugar in heavy skillet, stirring well until it reaches the brown caramel stage. When both mixtures are ready, carefully add caramel to first mixture, stirring with a long-handled spoon. Cook to soft ball stage; remove from heat and cool to lukewarm. Add vanilla, nuts, butter and salt, and beat until stiff and creamy. Drop onto buttered marble slab or buttered cookie sheet. Makes twenty 3-inch pralines.

Like Thomas Jefferson, Benjamin Franklin was a man of many interests and many talents. He founded the American Philosophical Society (which is still in operation) as well as the first subscription library in the United States. He organized the first fire department, and he instigated programs to pave Philadelphia's streets, clean them and light them. He helped found the University of Pennsylvania and the first hospital in Philadelphia. When he saw that the postal system was slow and inefficient, he took the job of Postmaster General. And along the way he invented the very efficient Franklin stove, and also became an expert printer, soap-maker, candle-maker and experimental farmer.

In 1752, he carried out his famous experiments with a kite, which indicated that lightning is electricity. He then invented the lightning rod. He studied and charted the Gulf Stream's course through the Atlantic Ocean, and he invented bifocal eye-glasses. He proposed daylight-saving time in summer, for he considered it wasteful that people were willing to "live much by candlelight and sleep by sunshine."

At 70, Franklin was the oldest signer of the Declaration of Independence. His name had by this time become a household word, because he published *Poor Richard's Almanac* annually from 1733 to 1758. Many of his wise and witty sayings are still frequently quoted —*Early to bed and early to rise, makes a man healthy, wealthy and wise. . . . He that falls in love with himself will have no rivals.*

After the Declaration of Independence was adopted, Congress appointed Franklin Minister to France. He helped draft the Treaty of Paris, which aided the cause of the American Revolution. Returning to his own country at the age of 81, he was responsible for the setting up, in the Constitution, of our two-house Congress.

Overleaf. *Carpenters' Hall, Philadelphia, Pennsylvania. This structure was built in 1770 as a meeting place for the city's carpenters, who had united to form a guild (the equivalent of a modern-day trade union). Delegates to the First Continental Congress met here in September of 1774 and, after much debate, passed a resolution calling for a total trade boycott against England. Many historic buildings dating from the Revolutionary period still stand in Philadelphia, including one that still serves as headquarters for the American Philosophical Society, founded by Benjamin Franklin in 1743.*

CHAPTER 16

Benjamin Franklin, Colonial Leader

A Patio Party

With all his seriousness, Franklin was also a man who lived life fully. At my summer patio party, I sometimes use a bust of this patriot as a centerpiece, on a blue-checked cloth. A paper-mâché Franklin stove filled with fresh flowers would also be appropriate for this theme. The menu is simple fare, suitable for casual entertaining.

A Benjamin Franklin Patio Party

Ben Franklin, one of the patriots who contributed greatly to the formation of our nation, continued to be a leader after the Revolution was won. In addition to helping draft the Declaration of Independence and the Constitution, he founded the first fire department, library, police department, hospital and post office.

Do Come to Our Party!

Date:

Time:

Place:

Casual Dress

RSVP

MENU

Philadelphia Horseradish Beef Rounds
Poor Richard Mushrooms

Franklin Green Salad   Mateus Crackling Rosé
Herbed French Dressing
Macaroni and Cheese Salad

Barbecued Spareribs   Mirassou Vineyards
                                  Gamay Beaujolais

Baked Idaho Potatoes
Baked Summer Squash

Cornbread Squares

Cranberry Crisp Delight   Sebastiani Vineyards
                                      Pinot Noir

Clockwise from center front: Barbecued Spareribs, Franklin Green Salad, Baked Idaho Potatoes. (Photographed at the home of Dr. and Mrs. Thomas Whitelock III. Antique table setting from the collection of Mr. Thorwald Jensen and the late Mrs. Jensen.)

Philadelphia Horseradish Beef Rounds

1 package (8 oz.) cream cheese
3 tsp. horseradish
1/8 tsp. onion salt
1/8 tsp. garlic salt
1 tsp. chopped parsley
Pinch paprika
1 package (8 oz.) sliced beef

Mix cheese with horseradish, onion salt, garlic salt and parsley. Spread on 6 slices of beef, placing one on top of another. Roll as neatly as possible and wrap in waxed paper. Chill several hours. Slice, sprinkle with paprika and serve on platter. Serves 8.

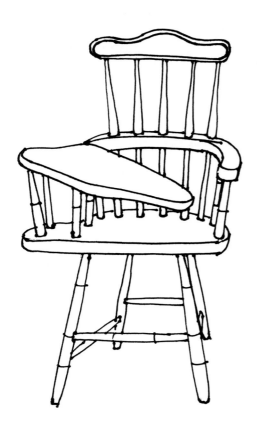

Poor Richard Mushrooms

1/2 cup water
1/4 cup butter
Dash salt
1/8 tsp. paprika
1/2 cup sifted all-purpose flour
2 eggs
Mushroom filling

Put water, butter, salt and paprika in a small saucepan and bring to a boil. Add flour all at once. Stir vigorously, cooking until mixture leaves sides of pan and forms a ball. Beat in eggs, one at a time. Continue to beat until mixture is thick and shiny. Shape little rounds of mixture (about 1 tsp. each), using two teaspoons, and place rounds 2 inches apart on ungreased baking sheet. Bake in preheated 450° oven for 15 minutes; lower heat to 350° and bake 20 minutes longer. Cool. Slit puffs on one side and fill with mushroom filling. Makes 4 dozen.

Filling:

1/2 lb. fresh mushrooms
1 T. butter
1 T. flour
1/4 cup heavy cream
1/4 cup rosé wine
1/4 cup chopped green onion tops
1/8 tsp. curry powder
Salt and pepper to taste

Discard stems from mushrooms. Chop caps fine and sauté with onions in butter for 5 minutes. Sprinkle flour evenly over mushrooms, then stir in cream and wine. Cook, stirring, over low heat until thickened. Add curry powder, salt and pepper. Makes enough for 4 dozen puffs.

Franklin Green Salad

1 head iceberg lettuce
1 head romaine lettuce
1 small head red cabbage
4 green onions, chopped (tops and bottoms)
1 cucumber, sliced

Wash vegetables. Break lettuce into small pieces, shred cabbage. Combine all ingredients and chill. Serve with Herbed French Dressing.

Herbed French Dressing

Mix 4 T. tarragon vinegar with ½ tsp. each salt and white pepper; add 1 cup olive oil and 3 T. minced tarragon. Beat the dressing until well combined.

Macaroni and Cheese Salad

Cook one package (7 oz.) elbow macaroni according to directions. Drain and rinse with cold water. Add 2½ T. tarragon vinegar, mix lightly. Allow to stand in refrigerator 15 minutes. Then add 1 cup diced mild Cheddar cheese, ½ cup chopped green pepper, ¼ cup diced celery, 2 T. chopped pimento, 3 T. minced green onion and ⅔ cup all-purpose dressing. Garnish with pimento strips. Serves 8.

Barbecued Spareribs

6 lbs. spareribs
1 tsp. dry mustard
½ tsp. salt
2 tsp. paprika
3 drops Tabasco sauce
2 T. Worcestershire sauce
2 T. honey
½ cup catsup
1 cup vinegar
1 cup water
¼ cup butter
2 cloves garlic, minced
2 onions, chopped

Cut spareribs into serving pieces, boil 20 minutes in water to cover, and cool. Combine remaining ingredients, bring to boil, and cool. Pour sauce over spareribs in a large bowl; marinate 2–3 hours, turning meat occasionally. Place ribs in pan, and roast in preheated 325° oven for 2 hours, turning and basting with marinade occasionally. Serves 6.

Baked Summer Squash

1 lb. fresh zucchini squash
1 lb. yellow squash
3 eggs, slightly beaten
2 T. sour cream
1 cup dry bread crumbs
1 cup grated Cheddar cheese
1 medium onion, chopped
2 T. butter, melted
½ tsp. salt
¼ tsp. garlic salt
¼ tsp. basil
¼ tsp. rosemary
¼ tsp. oregano

Coarsely grate unpeeled squashes. Combine eggs, sour cream, bread crumbs and cheese. Add remaining ingredients and squash. Place mixture in 9x12x2-inch loaf pan, and bake at 375° for 45 minutes. Cut into squares and serve. Serves 8.

Cranberry Crisp Delight

2 cups fresh cranberries
1 lb. cooking apples, peeled, cored and
    coarsely chopped
1 cup granulated sugar
1½ cup quick-cooking rolled oats
1 cup firmly packed light brown sugar
½ cup butter
½ tsp. salt
Vanilla ice cream

Combine cranberries, apples and granulated sugar. Turn into a buttered 9-inch pie pan. With pastry blender or finger tips, work together the rolled oats, brown sugar, butter and salt to make a crumbly mixture. Sprinkle over fruit. Bake in a preheated 350° oven for 1 hour. Serve warm, topped with ice cream. Serves 8.

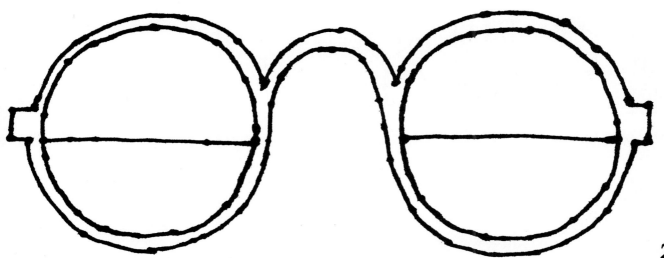

213

"If you spent the evening in a tavern," wrote John Adams, "you found it full of people drinking drams of flip, carousing, and swearing. The old taprooms were certainly cheerful and inviting gathering places."

So imagine, if you will, that you have mounted your sturdy steed and are setting out for a full day's journey in colonial times. It is late December, and snow is beginning to fall. You shiver inside your warm woolen cloak, while your horse plods steadily onward across the countryside. As the day's ride nears its end, you glimpse the edge of a village. Only a short distance farther, beyond a row of two-story white houses and a tall-spired little church, is the common—and Mr. Ebenezer Craft's Public House.

The stable boy takes your horse to the barn after you dismount, and you enter the lobby of the inn. The welcoming innkeeper invites you to sign the Night Register, and the warmth of a crackling fire takes the winter chill from your bones. Luckily, you are the first to arrive, so you will have the inn's only private room all to yourself. As you climb the steep and narrow staircase to the room, you see that the cooks have filled the great fireplace with black iron kettles of stew and vegetables, in anticipation of a "full house." Bread is rising in the oven, and the aroma of meats and vegetables fills the air.

Every village in the colonies had a tavern inn, where travelers were provided with lodging, food and drink. For the businessman, inns were the centers of colonial life, where important decisions were made over glasses of ale or wine. Inns were used as meeting houses, as court rooms, as hospitals—and sometimes even as prisons and as army barracks.

Although many inns were owned by women, women guests were not welcome. (Accommodations were sometimes crowded, and travelers slept three or four to a bed.) Evenings were relaxed and many parlor games were played, billiards being the most popular. The Yankee cuisine included fresh vegetables, usually grown on the inn's grounds. Meat was often preserved by smoking, salting or pickling.

There are still inns—either restored or maintained—waiting for your visit throughout the old colonial region. The Country Inns, as they are called today, are charming places, often lit by flickering candlelight and the flames of an open fire. You can capture this atmosphere with an intimate cheese and wine tasting party in your home. I try to keep these parties small, and reflective of a colonial mood. A bonus is that the food and drink are easy to prepare.

Overleaf. *City Tavern, Philadelphia, Pennsylvania. During the meetings of the Continental and Federal Congresses held in Philadelphia, City Tavern was the scene of many after-hours receptions and banquets. Shown here is the dining room of the reconstructed colonial social center, which is located in Independence Hall National Historical Park.*

CHAPTER 17

The Tavern Inn

A Wine and Cheese Tasting Party

Select four or five cheeses, ranging from mild to sharp and from creamy smooth to firm. Also consider contrasts in color and shape. Then select an equal numer of wines, from mild to robust. I allow about half a pound of cheese and at least a third of a bottle of wine for each guest.

Have cheeses at room temperature, to allow their true flavors to emerge. Take them out of the refrigerator about forty-five minutes before serving.

For wine tasting, provide a pitcher of distilled water so guests can rinse out their glasses between wines—along with a container for the rinse water. (If you have enough glasses to provide clean ones for each wine, this is not necessary—but few of us have this extensive a supply of glassware.)

Begin with the mild cheeses and mellow wines, progressing to sharp cheeses and robust vintages. Serve the Tavern Fondue and also offer unsalted biscuits (English crackers), unsalted pecan halves and apple slices, so that guests can clear their palates between tastings. We have fun discussing the various wines, and sometimes I supply score cards. If you offer an aperitif, or white or rosé or sparkling wines, do serve them chilled (for at least 3 hours in the refrigerator).

So break open the champagne, and let's get on with our Tavern Inn Party!

FOLD

PRINT
INFO INSIDE

CUT
OUT SPAPE

1776

Come to Our Tavern Inn . . .

. . . for an evening of wine and cheese tasting. We intend to make it a good old-fashioned evening, similar to those that were celebrated in colonial times. Please come to our party!

Date:

Time:

Place:

RSVP

MENU

Tavern Fondue

Cheeses

Apple Slices

Toasted Pecans

Wines

Assorted Cheeses and Wines, and Tavern Fondue. (Antiques courtesy of the Snow Goose Shoppe, La Jolla, California.)

Score Card

Name _____

Name of Wine					
Appearance 2					
Color 2					
Bouquet & Color 4					
Sugar 2					
Body 2					
Flavor 4					
General Quality 2					
TOTAL					

Scoring Totals

Wine Tasting Evaluation Sheet

17 to 20, wines must have some outstanding characteristic and no marked defect; 13 to 16, standard wines with neither an outstanding character or defect; 9 to 12, wines of commercial acceptability, but with a noticeable defect; 5 to 8, wines of below commercial acceptability; 1 to 4, completely spoiled wines.

Tavern Fondue

1 lb. Swiss cheese, grated
½ lb. Gruyere cheese, grated
Flour
Vin de Neuchatel
Dash each nutmeg and freshly ground
   pepper
Hard French bread cubes

In a fondue pot that has been rubbed with fresh garlic, place the cheeses, which have been dusted with a bit of flour. Add nutmeg and pepper. As the cheese starts to melt, add the wine, stirring constantly. Be careful not to burn the fondue; keep warm over burner of fondue pot. With long fondue forks, spear bread cubes and dip into the fondue.

Here are some compatible cheeses and wines, good selections for this kind of party:

Cheese	Wine	Specific Wine
Blue and Gorgonzola	Claret, Burgundy, port brandy Chianti	Beringer Burgundy
Brie	Port, cognac, calvados	Hennessey Cognac
Brick	Rosé, white wine sherry	Pinot Chardonnay
Camembert	Port, sherry, Madeira, claret, Burgundy	California Cabernet Sauvignon
Cream	Sparkling wines, rosés	Lancers Sparkling Rosé
Edam	Tokay, claret	Gamay Beaujolais
Gouda	Tokay, rosé	German Cold Duck
Liederkranz and Limburger	Dry red wines	Petite Sarah
Monterey Jack and Muenster	Rosés, white wines, Cream sherry	Chenin Blanc
Neufchatel	Sparkling wines, rosés, white wines	Neuchatel, Swiss
Swiss	Sauterne, champagne, dry or sweet white wine, sparkling Burgundy	Extra dry Champagne

Entertainment by P. PATTON

When the Federal Convention met at Philadelphia in 1787 to frame the Constitution, George Washington was unanimously voted presiding officer. The Convention issued this revealing statement, "Tho we cannot, affirmatively, tell you what we are doing, we can negatively, tell you what we are not doing; we never once thought of a King."

The new Constitution called for the election of a President. George Washington and the Presidents who have followed him have not been elected directly by a vote of the people, however, but by members of the Electoral College. In the first Presidential election, held in February of 1789, Washington was elected President by unanimous vote of the College.

New York City was then the capitol of our country, and throngs of citizens watched as Washington rode in a horse-drawn coach to Federal Hall on Inauguration Day. After he was sworn in, a 13-gun salute was fired, one for each colony.

This was the beginning of representative government, and Election Day remains a fine opportunity for celebrating with friends. I decorate my house with red-white-and-blue bunting, and some years I ask guests to dress in these colors.

It's not necessary, I've found, to restrict your guest list to one particular political party. One year I invited everyone who lived on our dead-end street—none of us knew each other except by sight. I made name tags identifying people as others recognized them: Camellia Grower, White Station Wagon, Fence Painter, and so on.

CHAPTER 18

Election Day

An Open House Party

It's a good idea to have television sets in separate rooms, one for each political party, with the food in a single separate location. Our mixed gatherings have never resulted in fights (although there have certainly been some heated discussions). Be sure to make enough food, because tension seems to increase appetites. The cocktail-dinner also extends for several hours. So set the table with chafing dishes and iced liners, to keep the food "going" all night. That way your guests will be able to serve themselves, as they feel like it. When finally the winners are announced, I bring on the Election Cake, along with a toast to the victors.

Election Night Open House
Hamilton Franklin Jefferson Washington
Adams Revere Hancock

The beginning of our freedom and the privilege of electing our own representatives was first celebrated in February of 1789, when electors voted George Washington our first President. Come help us celebrate this event!

Date:

Time:

Place:

RSVP

MENU

Suggested Wines:

Hot Cheese Dip
Blue Cheese Wheel
Cheddar Cheese Bits
Artichoke-Ham Bites
Carrot Sticks
Election Appetizers
Lomi Salmon Appetizers
Watercress-Spinach Salad Bowl with Garlic French Dressing
Molded Waldorf Salad
Tuna Parfait
Seafood Medley
Parsleyed Rice
Deviled Cheese Bread

Old Hartford Election Cake

Coffee

Taylor New York State
Extra Dry Champagne

Lillet French
Apéritif

Clockwise from upper right: Old Hartford Election Cake, Deviled Cheese Bread, Lomi Salmon Polly Allen, Cheddar Cheese Bits, Carrot Sticks, Seafood Medley.

Hot Cheese Dip

10 oz. extra sharp Cheddar cheese, shredded
10 oz. Swiss cheese, shredded
2 T. flour
⅔ cup white wine
1 T. prepared mustard
⅛ tsp. garlic salt
Bite-sized Nabisco Shredded Wheat
French bread cubes

Shred cheeses, add flour and toss lightly until cheese is coated. In a medium saucepan, heat wine, mustard and garlic salt over low heat. Do not boil. Add one-fourth of the cheese and stir until it melts. Continue to add cheese in quarters, stirring until melted after each addition. When all of cheese has been added, remove mixture to chafing dish to keep warm. With forks or toothpicks, dip shredded wheat or French bread cubes into the fondue. Makes 2½ cups.

Artichoke-Ham Bites

Drain 1 can artichoke hearts and cut in half. Marinate in ½ cup garlic-flavored Italian dressing several hours; drain. Cut one 6-oz. package smoked sliced ham in 1½-inch strips. Wrap 1 strip around each artichoke. Spear with frilled red-and-blue toothpicks. Bake at 300° for 10 minutes. Serve hot.

Election Appetizers

2 cups sifted flour
½ tsp. salt
3 tsp. baking powder
¼ cup shortening
⅔ cup grated Cheddar cheese
⅔ cup milk

Sift flour, salt and baking powder into a bowl. Cut shortening in with a fork. Add grated cheese, then milk, Chill dough. Divide into two parts. Roll each into a 6x12-inch rectangle. Spread each portion with half the filling, then roll as for a jelly roll (starting at long side). Cut in slices 1-inch thick. Bake at 450° on greased cookie sheet for 12–15 minutes.

Filling:

1 lb. lean ground beef
¼ cup minced onion
2 T. minced green pepper
2 T. butter
2 T. chili sauce
½ tsp. salt
¼ tsp. seasoned pepper

Fry meat until browned. Sauté onion and green pepper in 2 T. butter. Add cooked meat and seasonings. For variations, use ham, chicken or lamb.

235

Lomi Salmon Appetizer

(Polly Allen)

1 can (7¾ oz.) salmon
6 green onions, chopped
2 or 3 medium tomatoes, chopped fine
Large cherry tomatoes

Remove skin and bones from salmon, chop or shred fine. Add onion and chopped tomatoes. Scoop out centers of cherry tomatoes and fill with salmon mixture. Serve on a bed of shredded lettuce. Makes 24.

Watercress-Spinach Salad Bowl

1 bunch watercress
1 head fresh spinach
1 head Bibb lettuce
4 T. grated Parmesan cheese
2 hard-cooked eggs
4 slices bacon, cooked crisp and crumbled
¼ tsp. seasoned pepper

Wash and dry greens, and break into bite-sized pieces. Mix in other ingredients gently. Serve with Garlic French Dressing.

236

Garlic French Dressing

Sprinkle 2 garlic cloves with 1½ tsp. salt and mince. With a mortar and pestle, mash garlic to a paste. Transfer to bowl, stir in 4 T. red wine vinegar and ½ tsp. pepper. Add ⅔ cup olive oil in a stream, beating until dressing is well mixed. Serves 4.

Molded Waldorf Salad

3 medium-sized apples
1 T. lemon juice
1 package (3 oz.) lemon gelatin
1 cup hot water
⅛ tsp. salt
½ cup mayonnaise
¾ cup diced celery
¾ cup chopped walnuts
½ cup whipping cream, whipped
Garnishes

Core apples but do not peel. Dice, then sprinkle with lemon juice to prevent darkening; set aside. Dissolve gelatin in hot water, chill until it has consistency of egg white. Add salt, blend in the mayonnaise (using a beater if necessary to mix thoroughly). Fold in the diced apples, celery, walnuts and whipped cream. Pour into a greased 5- or 6-cup ring mold. To serve, unmold on a bed of salad greens. Garnish with apple wedges and whipped cream. Serves 6.

Tuna Parfait

2 envelopes unflavored gelatin
1 cup cold water
1 cup boiling water
1 cup mayonnaise
½ cup chili sauce
Lemon juice
Dash salt
2 cans (7 oz. each) tuna, flaked
½ cup chopped celery
½ cup pimento-stuffed green olives, sliced
Hard-cooked eggs

Soften gelatin in cold water; dissolve in boiling water. Cool. Combine mayonnaise, chili sauce, lemon juice and salt. Stir in the gelatin and mix well. Chill until partially set. Stir in tuna, celery and olives. Pour into 1½-quart melon mold; chill until firm. Unmold on crisp lettuce. Serve with hard-cooked eggs. Serves 8.

Seafood Medley

1 lb. fresh mushrooms, sliced
3 T. butter
4 T. butter
4 T. flour
½ tsp. salt
¼ tsp. white pepper
½ tsp. paprika
2 cups milk
½ cup white wine
½ lb. shrimp, cooked
½ lb. crab meat, cooked
½ lb. lobster meat, cooked
2 T. chopped chives

Sauté mushrooms in a small pan, using the 3 T. butter. In a separate pan, make a white wine sauce by melting the 4 T. butter, adding flour and seasonings, then gradually adding the wine. Add seafood, mushrooms and chives. Simmer, do not boil, until thoroughly hot. Serves 6.

Toasted Cheese Bread

1 loaf French bread, sliced in half lengthwise
½ cup (1 cube) butter
2 T. chopped parsley
1 cup grated Tillamook cheese
4 T. Parmesan cheese
2 tsp. dried chives
1 tsp. Worcestershire sauce
⅛ tsp. paprika
⅛ tsp. garlic powder
Dash celery salt

Combine and blend butter, parsley, cheese, chives and seasonings. Spread each slice of bread with mixture. Bake at 350° for 15–20 minutes to heat through. Slice and serve. Serves 8.

Old Hartford Election Cake

Raised Dough:

½ yeast cake
½ cup lukewarm water
1 T. butter
1 T. granulated sugar
¼ tsp. salt
1¼ cup flour

Dissolve yeast in water; add butter, sugar, salt and flour. Mix well, and set aside in warm place to rise until double in bulk (about 1½ hours).

Cake Batter:

½ cup butter
1 cup sugar
3 eggs, well beaten
¾ cup raisins
¼ cup sliced citron
1 tsp. grated lemon rind
1½ tsp. lemon juice
¾ tsp. baking soda
¾ cup flour
¼ tsp. nutmeg
½ cup brandy

Cream together butter and sugar, and beat until light. Add eggs, raisins, citron, lemon rind and lemon juice. Sift together baking soda, flour and nutmeg, and add alternately with brandy to creamed mixture.

Combine raised dough and batter, and pour into well-greased bread pan. Let rise in warm place for about 1 hour. Bake in a preheated 350° oven for 1 hour. Ice while still warm, with Royal Icing.

Royal Icing:

Sift 1 lb. confectioner's sugar onto waxed paper, twice. In a bowl, combine 2 egg whites lightly with juice of 1 lemon. Gradually mix sugar into egg-white mixture with wooden spoon. Add only enough sugar to make a creamy, smooth, thinly spreadable icing. Use metal spatula dipped in water to spread icing over cake. To obtain a high glaze, let first layer of icing dry and then apply a second layer.

241

Liquid Measures

American (Standard Cup)

1 cup = ½ pint = 8 fl. oz.
1 T. = ½ fl. oz.
1 tsp. = 1/6 fl. oz.
1 pint = 16 fl. oz.
1 quart = 2 pints = 32 fl. oz.

Metric Equivalent

2.37 deciliter (dl.)
1.5 centiliter (cl.)
0.5 cl.
4.73 dl.
9.46 dl.

Solid Measures

American

1 lb. = 16 oz.
2.2 lbs.
1 oz.
3½ oz.

Metric Equivalent

453 grams
1000 grams = 1 kilogram
28 grams
100 grams

Oven Temperatures

Farenheit

Up to 225°	Cool
225-275°	Very slow
275-325°	Slow
350-375°	Moderate
400-450°	Hot
450-500°	Very hot
500°	Extremely hot

Centigrade

Up to 105°
105-135°
135-160°
175-190°
215-230°
230-260°
260°

Conversion Tables

Index